CW01314547

OCCUPATION NAVIGATION

THE ULTIMATE CAREER GUIDE FOR
YOUNG PROFESSIONALS

JAMES D. BROWNE

This publication is designed to provide competent and reliable information regarding the subject matter covered. However, it is sold with the understanding that the author and publisher are not engaged in rending legal, financial, or other professional advice. Laws and practices often vary from country to country and district to province and if legal or other expert assistance is required, the services of a professional should be sought. The author and publisher specifically disclaim any liability that is incurred from the use or application of the contents of this book.

Copyright © James D Browne 2020

James D Browne has asserted his right to be identified as the author of this work in accordance with the Copyright, Design and Patents Act 1988.

A CIP catalogue record for this book is available from the British Library.

All rights reserved. No part of this publication may be reproduced, stored in a retrieval system, or transmitted in any form or by any means, electronic, mechanical, photocopying, recording or otherwise, without the prior permission of the copyright owner.

Published in 2020 by Occupation Navigation Limited. Addresses and details for Occupation Navigation can be found at www.occupationnavigation.co.uk. Printed and bound by KDP publishing.

At Occupation Navigation Ltd, environmental consciousness is important to us. Our ink is chlorine-free, and our acid-free interior paper stock is supplied by a Forest Stewardship Council-certified provider. In addition, our paper is made from 30% post-consumer waste recycled material. We also maintain a commitment to recycling waste materials resulting from the printing process and from daily office operations, and we will continue to review our practices to ensure we are doing our part to protect the environment.

ISBN 9798639000584

OCCUPATION NAVIGATION

For my mentors.

For all my colleagues throughout the years.

Thank you for everything.

CONTENTS

Preface i

1. Introduction 1

2. Laying The Foundations 15

3. Vision 39

4. Career Planning 63

5. Gaining An Edge 75

6. Interviews & Applications 105

7. Negotiations 143

8. Workplace Relationships 165

9. Health 101 177

10. Networking 213

11. Mentors 233

12. Staying Motivated 245

13. Conclusion 259

Preface

This book was inspired by my friends and colleagues over the years. Those who worked the hardest without seeing the results they deserved. Everyone who's felt overlooked and over worked. This book aims to be everything you need. A condensed version of 10,000 different resources you might read to draw the same conclusions. Everything in this book is tried and tested across multiple industries. Everything unnecessary has been removed. The aim here has been to distil the best wisdom and knowledge on all matters career related into an engaging, readable book anyone can benefit from. I'm pleased to say that goal has been achieved in publishing this work.

I've wanted to write this book for a long time. When I started out in my career, I would have found it immensely valuable to have the resources I needed to succeed available in one place. At the time I wasn't sure what those resources were. I didn't know what I didn't know. To have had everything I needed in a single reliable book would have changed my life and saved me a lot of time trying to climb my ladder. Throughout my career, I was fortunate enough to encounter great minds and have highly successful mentors show me the way forward. I was blessed to go on to achieve a very high level of financial success very early in my life. I continued to rise through the ranks in my career. Unfortunately, I found myself leaving my friends and peers behind. I realised not everyone had the opportunity to work with great leaders and learn the vital lessons early.

In this book I distil the lessons you need to know to reach new levels of success in your career. This guide to career success for young professionals was put together with knowledge from industry leaders, professionals from all fields and my own personal experience. This book is based in the real world and is a practical, usable guidebook to navigate your way to total career mastery. The lessons here will give you the tools you need to build the life you want.

Until now it just hasn't existed. Sure, you'll find a myriad of self-help books on every topic imaginable from influencing people to building wealth and the like. These books aren't always based in reality, and often don't offer the clear, practical advice necessary. I'm a big fan of TED talks, podcasts and articles. Many of these resources are useful in their own right. You can spend hours, days and weeks trawling through this content to find a few hidden gems. In this book we present the hard facts and essential information from the best of the best. There is a lack of credible, pragmatic advice for young professionals in a succinct format. This book is here to redress the balance and bring together the collective learning from the brightest minds on the subject in one place.

Chapter 1

Introduction

The year is 2016. It's Monday morning, 8am. The long week stretches ahead of me like a marathon I haven't trained for. Damn, more like a marathon I didn't even sign up for. I've just lost my job as a Relationship Manager for one of the UK's largest banks. My day now consists of processing digital paperwork in a back office and trying not to think about whether this is all there is to life. How did I get here? After all I've always worked hard. In my head, things like this don't happen to hard working people. How could it be that things had gone so badly wrong? I had visions of moving back into my parents' house, resentful and defeated, beaten by the cruel world. Woe was me.

So how did things go from this situation, to me getting my first area management position and buying my first home before that year was over? The truth is that it wasn't that complicated. Once I'd realised where I was going wrong, learned the hard lessons and applied them,

INTRODUCTION

things started to improve. Since that time, I've seen unbelievable success in my career, started several businesses, travelled and met the most incredible people. I don't have a university degree, I left school at 17 without much in the way of formal qualifications. If you have those things that's fantastic. However, let's dispel a common myth from the outset; with the obvious exceptions aside (medical doctors, academics, the like) you do *not* need an advanced formal education to be a success in your career.

We're going to work together throughout this book to build a vision of the life you want and then to achieve it. This is a practical guide based in the real world. Everything you read is tested and works. It's worked for me, my esteemed peers and industry leaders, and (most probably) your current managing director. It's no big secret, in fact I encourage you to share the message far and wide.

We're going to try and set you up with the best life possible. There are some important steps to get there. We're trying to enjoy the process and live a good life right now. That life needs to move you upwards towards something better. When I worked in financial services I learned about the concept of compound interest. The idea is simple. Imagine I give you a 1 pence coin that doubles in value every day. After a month (31 days), that penny is worth over £10 million. Do the math quickly if you don't believe this. It's growing at the same rate (doubling) but the results come very slowly at first then more and more rapidly as time goes on. Now imagine that the 1 pence coin is your current level of communication skills, negotiation skills, self-confidence, personal brand, health, etc. Making small regular investments in yourself and your skills will yield massive results over time.

This book will allow you to identify your areas of strength and weakness. Done honestly and critically this will give us a firm basis to start building the sort of life you want. You'll be amazed how quickly you can see results. However, please do not think this is a "get rich quick" book. This is a book that advocates setting your life up correctly and living well, thereby becoming a strong person of the most value to the people around you. Doing this will facilitate your success better than any quick tips. The advice contained in this book is worth its weight in gold when implemented correctly, but it's all for nothing if you're not able to hold up the weight of your own success.

Let's take a look at some key indicators of success to see what we can learn.

IQ – This is the first indicator of success, and it's worth discussing. IQ stands for intelligence quotient and is the most widely accepted way of measuring general intelligence that humanity has currently devised. IQ exams work by testing you and giving you a score, which will tell you roughly how intelligent you happen to be. The average IQ score across the population is always 100. As average intelligence levels increase or decrease the average remains the same at 100. It's important to say this isn't the only measure of intelligence, and some people dispute the validity of IQ tests. This is fair enough. Just know it is the most widely accepted measure of individual intelligence and people with higher IQ scores are more likely to see career success on average. It's this way because the test results are based on how well you individually compare to everyone else. Within the field of IQ you have a split between fluid IQ and crystallised IQ. Fluid roughly approximating your ability to abstract and think quickly, crystallised being more a measure of how much information you currently know. There's some debate on whether or not you can actually increase your IQ, with the research seemingly indicating it is relatively fixed. A lot of the controversy around IQ stems from this issue. For our purposes however, the fact you've picked up this book and are aiming at a better life indicates that you are a smart person with the mental resources necessary to move upwards. You don't need to be a genius, hardly anyone is. Genius' account for roughly 0.03% of the population, and you'll need an IQ score of at least 150. IQ distribution means that the majority of everyone (almost 70%) fall within 1 standard deviation of the norm. Meaning somewhere between a score of 85 and 115. The bell curve graph on the following page illustrates the distribution of IQ scores in the general population.

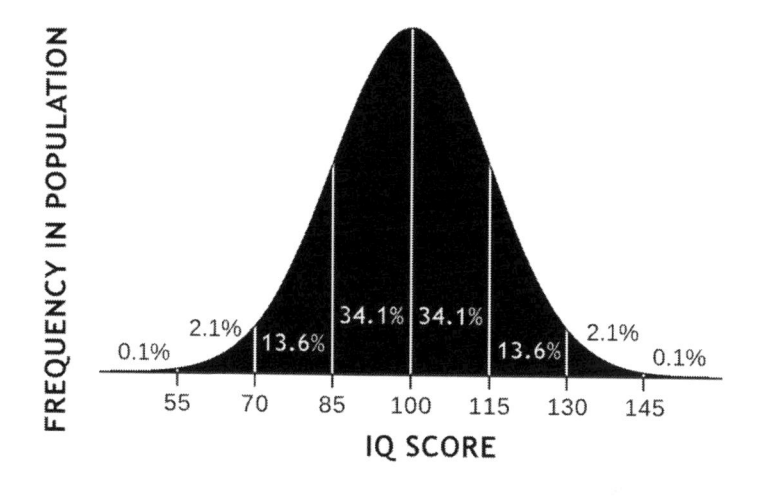

The literature on this outlines that your fluid IQ will decline with age. For this reason, IQ tests are adjusted for age. This just means that if you do take one at 50, you'll need to answer less questions correctly than someone who is 20 to get the same score. Interestingly your crystallised IQ can and should continue to increase with age. This makes sense because you learn things and accrue more knowledge during your lifetime in theory. The best way to maintain your fluid IQ level with age is to look after your body. Your brain uses a huge amount of oxygen to function so healthy lungs and cardiovascular systems help prevent the brain from having to slow down so much in older age. Provided you're not still a child, statistically speaking you're the smartest you'll ever be today, right now. Make the most of that and commit to finishing this book and taking the actions needed to build the life you want. It will never be easier than it is right now.

INTRODUCTION

It's important to understand that lots of people who do remarkable things are not extraordinarily intelligent. The average celebrity IQ is around 107, whilst this is slightly above average it is not remarkable. There are notable people of influence in popular culture with IQ scores below 100. It pays to understand IQ well to make sure it doesn't hold you back. If you have a high IQ this will make some things easier for you, if you don't, you'll have to work slightly harder – but as with everything, the reverse can also be true under the right conditions.

In today's poplar psychology IQ often gets discussed together with emotional intelligence. So, you may expect us to discuss emotional intelligence also, which we will in some regards throughout this book. However, do not confuse IQ with emotional intelligence. They are entirely separate fields. My personal opinion could be that they're both important in different regards though the research literature is clear that they do not carry equal weight as predictors of success. With this said, there are some specific characteristics of emotional intelligence which influence success, and we will discuss those later on.

The next indicator of success is a personality trait known as conscientiousness. Let's define the term. If you're naturally conscientious, you'll be hard working and prefer order in your life. The sort of person who generally remembers where they put their keys and is able to get up at the same time every morning would be described as conscientious. You might ask why these people are more likely to be successful, and besides the reasons that are obvious (the time you waste looking for keys could probably be better spent working on something productive) there are some interesting ideas worth exploring hidden in here.

Not everyone is an instinctively conscientious person. I have to work hard to remain motivated and keep myself on track in everything I do. I keep meaningful personalised goals that I'm working on at any given time. This gives my life meaning and structure and makes it easier to stay on the right path. We will of course discuss how the industry leaders and other people you look up to set their goals and stay motivated. For now, understand that conscientiousness is a predictor of success. However, if you're not waking up at 5.30am every day with endless energy and motivation, that's just fine and completely normal - and we all still lose our keys every now and then too.

A word on motivation and success. It's important to understand that motivation is not a fixed or permanent thing. It is a feeling and state of mind, and as such will intensify and diminish with the flow of many things that are outside of your immediate control. Have some compassion and understanding for yourself here. We are going to set your life up so that you're able to stay on the right path but know that nobody wakes up feeling amazing every single morning. Overly positive celebrity interviews, the impact of filtered lives on social media and such like have projected an unobtainable standard of wellbeing into the public consciousness. Even if we don't consume this material ourselves, everyone around us does and continues to project that standard of wellbeing onto us. Some people are genuinely going through difficult times and that should be seen as alright, in fact struggle and pain are intrinsically part of life. Societally, we're increasingly seeing this as not ok, that perhaps there's something wrong with us. This is not saying this is just the media's fault. It's just not obvious that someone who's bereaved, has lost a job or is battling a painful illness is mentally ill. A label of mental illness suggests the problem is inside the individual when this just isn't always the case. Diagnosis of depression is at an all-time high in the UK and much of the western world. Perhaps sometimes the mental illness we call depression is a perfectly natural response to extremely challenging conditions. Perhaps it shouldn't be labelled as an illness so quickly in these cases. There's a huge stigma around not staying motivated and hustling away 24/7. Do not assume that if you're not motivated 24/7 that there's something wrong with you. We all must deal with tragedy when it arrives, and it will arrive. We could learn to treat ourselves with the same compassion we would treat a close friend or loved one in the same situation as ourselves. You wouldn't expect them to just get on with it and be disappointed when they don't just carry on as normal, and to suggest that sounds uncompassionate. It's just as important we don't place unrealistic expectations on ourselves. You will get where you want to be much faster and enjoy the process much more if you're reasonable with yourself and those around you about what to expect from yourself.

Here's something to consider; free advice is usually worth exactly what you pay for it. Everyone you know, your parents, your teachers, your friend who works in the coffee shop for minimum wage, they all think they know what you should do with your life. Easy for them to say. Unless these people have achieved the level of great success in life you're looking for, you should probably stop listening. Nobody should decide what you do with your life except you. It's tragic to see 40-year-old children, following a path laid out for them by someone else years ago. It lays the foundations for a mid-life crisis. This often happens when people realise they're half way through life and haven't done enough of anything meaningful or worthwhile. People with beautiful families and a Porsche in the driveway aren't immune to this phenomenon. We're going to make sure this doesn't happen to you. We ridicule the cliched mid-life crisis in pop culture but in reality, it's a tragedy that levels people. Our world is full of over-educated worker bees, never waking up to their full potential. To be hit with that reality after expending your precious youth is too much for some people to bare. So, this is an invitation to wake up and face the truth of the situation. Nobody can decide what you should do with your life except you. I'm going to say that again. Nobody can decide what you should do with your life, except you. You're going to have to decide whether you want to work behind a desk or eat meat or believe in God and so on for infinity.

How do you decide what to do about the most important issues? Shouldn't you listen to the advice of people around you, especially if you trust them? After all, your family probably love you and want what's best for you. Maybe you still think your parents are all knowing and actually know much better than you? Why might you believe that? After all it's pure chance that your parents are who they are. You probably have friends with parents, and you likely value your own parent's opinion more highly than you value other parent's opinions. Why is that? After all our parents surely aren't actually the most informed, educated and wise people. Under different circumstances we might have been born to one of our friend's parents, and we would then see them the same way. During your mid-twenties (or when you leave the nest to establish your own life) you should transition to having a relationship with your parents approximating highly respected peers. You value their council equally to other people with approximately their level of experience and success. This doesn't mean you love them any less. It means you fully realised they are the wonderful flawed people we all are, with no super powers that are unique to them as the people who created you. Perhaps you object to this on religious grounds, feeling like this would be dishonouring your parents. I can understand this growing up in a culture founded based on Judeo-Christian beliefs. After all the fifth commandment is "Honour thy father and mother". If this applies to you, understand that almost all religious scholars read that as respect, not worship. They reserve worship and absolute obedience for the all-powerful God.

We all must learn to think critically and make our own choices. We are creatures with desires, instincts and ambitions. Your individual desires might be similar to those of other people, but they are uniquely your own in important ways. For example, lots of people have the instinctive desire to have children, but the unique element is how many children, when you have them in life, and how much of your own life you want to dedicate to raising them personally. Many people desire lots of money, some for power, some for material luxury, some for security for their family. The point is you're a unique individual. What makes your parents or friends happy won't necessarily work for you, particularly if it isn't true to who you really are and what your true-self desires. You have these longings inside of you whether you consciously recognise and articulate them or not. If you don't listen to your true self and work to manifest it in the world, it will catch up to you. Probably around 40, or worse when you're much older. You need to respect yourself and your own desires at least as much as you do other people's (parents, friends, etc), and because it's your own life you must always have the final say on what you do. No, you don't need to take that particular promotion you don't want if it will make you miserable. No, you don't have to get that degree in a subject you don't love because someone made you believe that "you need a degree to do well". You'll come out the other side 3 years older and with debt and a career ahead of you in something you couldn't care less about. Maybe that doesn't sound so bad to you? People have always worked hard doing things they didn't like to provide for their families, right? True. However, in today's world it's a choice. Up until very recently it wasn't a choice, you worked in the fields 14 hours a day because if you didn't, you'd starve. People lived and died that way for thousands of years to advance the human race to where we are today. Today we have access to the whole of human knowledge at our fingertips whenever we need it (smart phones), along with the ability to contact anyone anywhere in the world instantly. We can travel around the world in hours without becoming bankrupt and dying of infectious diseases in the process. We always have enough to eat. Neighbouring countries have stopped trying to invade, conquer and enslave us. Even the ruling elites of yesteryear still didn't have antibiotics and died of winter chest infections at 52, when they weren't assassinated for their money and power. People lived and died for thousands of years in conditions we can't even imagine to build the world we live in today. We're so damned ungrateful and blind to everything the previous generations did for us. Things have never been better than they are right now. To not live up to your potential is optional in today's world. I can think of nothing that shows better gratitude than giving to the next generation what our forefathers gave to us, a better world. No one expects miracles from us as individuals, but everyone working to become the best person they can individually be changes the world for the better. We should do this for ourselves now and for the next generation. This isn't naïve either, we know people still experience real suffering. Maybe your boiler is broken, or your relationship is in a bad way, perhaps you have a handicap or illness, perhaps you're dealing with the hardest part of life – the death of someone you love. These are real problems. Your suffering and pain are real and you deserve some genuine sympathy. All I'm advocating is a larger perspective on human existence. Forever before us people faced the same issues in absolute poverty with no healthcare, warm water or safe shelter so that you could have these things today. Recognise these incredible things and work to maintain and protect them, perhaps even to make things better.

"A society grows great when old men plant trees whose shade they know they shall never sit in." – Proverb of Ancient Greece.

As you're reading a book for young professionals, you're likely in your 20's or 30's. In any case you've probably made some good and some bad decisions in your life so far. How is it working out for you? Maybe you don't know if you're on the right path because you're not walking towards anything in particular. That's all ok. We've just been exploring the core ideas that will allow us to understand what makes people successful. In brief; be smart about it, work hard, bad shit happens to everyone, keep putting one foot in front of the other, and just realise you have a better chance of success than anyone in human history ever. That's all well and good, now we can get into the practical stuff. In the next chapter we're going to explore how to lay the foundations for a successful life.

Chapter 2
Laying the Foundations

Before we go any further, we need to outline a few things. Some timeless wisdom that must be adopted before true meaning and success can be found in life. Get your mind right. Nobody is going to hand you anything you haven't worked for; nobody owes you anything. You have to develop yourself into the sort of person that can attain higher goals. Practically speaking, you can have anything you want in life. You just have to know how to demand it from the world and make the change in your life necessary to manifest what you want. You will have to sacrifice things to achieve your ambitions. The journey will be difficult but will reward you with what you actually want from life, provided you're aiming at the right thing and you keep moving forward. The difficulties will give you meaning in your life, and it will be worth it. Now we've set the frame we can start working on the practical things that will allow you to build yourself into the type of person capable of achieving great things.

Routine. Routines are essential for our wellbeing and make us functional people in the world. You cannot be mentally healthy without a routine. You need to simplify and structure the things in your life you do every day so that they become manageable. You cannot take over the world if all your underwear is sitting unwashed in the laundry basket. Nobody is going to give you new opportunities at work if you're 5 minutes late 3 times a month because you couldn't get yourself together and leave the house on time. If you don't eat breakfast or skip lunch, you're going to exhaust your mental faculties by 2pm, be less productive, make mistakes and have less patience to deal with difficult people. Now imagine you go to work everyday well rested and calm, your day planned out properly and realistic in its intentions, you're able to deal with everyone fairly and equally (even the ones you really don't like), you're highly productive and your managers and peers are continuously praising you for your excellent work. Which version of you is more likely to get the next promotion? It may seem comically obvious, but we're not very good at looking after ourselves.

We seem to think we're capable of telling ourselves what to do, and are continually surprised when we don't listen to our own orders. You know this if you've ever joined a gym and promised to go 3 times a week, or told yourself that you'll definitely start eating healthier, or promised yourself you'll never drink again after the worst hangover ever. You are not your own slave. You have a nature.

The part of you that thinks it's you, the part we call consciousness, makes up a very small percentage of your overall brain. You can't consciously force control over the parts of your brain that regulate your heart beat or body temperature, you have to work with them. An important point is this - it's the same with your will power or self-control. You can't will yourself to just stop being angry, you can't will yourself to just be satisfied all the time, you can't will yourself to function normally on 3 hours of sleep each night. Better to think of yourself as the captain of a ship who must negotiate with his crew. Captain being your consciousness or the part of you that thinks. The ship being your whole self and physical body. The crew being your will power, temperament and personality. The Captain must work with their crew to keep the ship in working order and moving forward in the right direction. The Captain must negotiate with the crew fairly and reward them appropriately for their contributions. A forceful approach with no regard for the crew's wellbeing will make them resentful and unlikely to follow orders. Machiavelli famously said in The Prince - "He who wishes to be obeyed must know how to command". Why would you assume you can treat yourself unreasonably and demand your own obedience in life like a tyrant? You need a routine, but you must reason with yourself when you create it and be willing to start small. Imagine telling your intimate partner that you'd thought things through quite carefully and have decided what would be best for them. They're to wake up at 5.00am every morning, go to the gym, cook themselves breakfast and make a fresh smoothie, wash up afterwards, shower, dress immaculately, meditate for 30 minutes, take a 45-minute walk to their full-time job and make sure they get there extra early at 8am. They're to work incredibly hard all day, maybe skipping lunch and leaving late. Once they're home around 6.30pm, they're to do the laundry, work on a creative project, attend yoga classes once a week, read 100 pages each night to get through their reading list, cook a healthy dinner and wash up afterwards and do some house work. They need to see friends or family at least 3 times a week too. Perhaps they have a pet or children to look after also, and they'll need to spend plenty of time with them. They'll also need to be in bed by 10.00pm to be well rested for the next day. You tell your partner their life isn't going the way they planned and they simply must do all these things otherwise they're a failure. What do you think your partner would say to that?

You would not assume anyone else would tolerate this from you. Not if they had any self-respect. So why on earth would we treat ourselves like this and expect ourselves to tolerate it? Who wants to work for a tyrant like that? And what are we giving ourselves in return for this round the clock prison of a schedule? We tell ourselves we'll be "healthier" and "successful one day"… good luck with that. No wonder we throw off those chains as quickly as possible, we skip breakfast and work half as hard when we know we shouldn't because at least that's temporary freedom from the shackles of our own tyranny.

So, how do we build a routine that's fair and that we would actually follow without growing bitter and resentful towards our good intentions, then throwing in the towel after a few weeks exhausted. After all we still have the slight problem that things need to be done, and we can't just sit around all day never achieving anything. We would grow equally bitter and resentful towards ourselves in that circumstance. The answer is to humble ourselves. We must have some respect for the fact we're not super human. Some people build incredibly productive routines and become very successful. Like all great things it won't happen instantly and requires patience. They say that behind every overnight success is years of hard work, and there's great wisdom in this. Start small and build something sustainable over time. You wouldn't try to fly a commercial airliner with no training, and that's roughly equivalent to trying to build a routine that will make you incredibly successful. It's something you're more than capable of that will take some time to master. You can learn to fly a commercial airliner within a flight simulator reasonably well within a few weeks, but there's a good reason why you need to bank 1500 flying hours before you'll get your pilots licence from the CAA or FAA. Great things take time, practice and patience to master. For all the reasons we've outlined above you cannot demand yourself to build and stick to a perfect ultra-productive routine from day one. Start from a humble place.

Where to start? The first thing to do is document what you usually do each day for one week. It doesn't need to be exact to every last detail it just needs to be honest. There's no point deceiving yourself with this because you'll just set yourself up to fail. Do this correctly and you'll be a massive step ahead. This really is the first thing you must do in real life to start moving towards the success you want. This will only take 30 minutes, so set aside the time and do it. Take a sheet of A4 and a pen. The paper should be orientated in landscape. Start by writing the days of the week along the top of the page. Down the left-hand side write Morning, Afternoon, Evening. Draw grid lines so you can see the three sections for each day. There's a small example for illustration purposes below. There is a larger, pre-completed example later in the chapter.

	Monday	Tuesday	Wednesday	Thursday	Friday	Saturday	Sunday
Morning							
Afternoon							
Evening							

For each day, document the following in each section. When you answer the questions below, try not to overthink it. This should be a quick exercise that isn't difficult. It doesn't need to be incredibly accurate, just write down the first honest answer the comes into your head. Don't waste any time here, just complete the exercise. If you work night shifts or otherwise don't fit into the typical working day, you may need to rearrange the categories below as appropriate. For example, if you typically wake up at 6pm to work your night shift and this is when you eat your first meal, move the questions that are typical to most people's morning section to your evening section on your grid.

Morning
05:00 – 12:00:

1. The time you wake up each day. If you don't wake up at a set time, state the latest time you're likely to get out of bed.

2. If you typically eat breakfast that day, and if so, what you usually eat.

3. Things you do before work that day, E.g.: Shower, Check social media for 15 minutes, jog for 20 minutes.

4. How you usually travel to work and how long it takes you.

5. The time you usually leave to go to work, if you work that day.

5a. If you're not working that day, state what you're likely to be doing with the time between waking up and midday. E.g.: Watching TV, Recovering from a hangover, Browsing Social Media on my smart phone, etc. Just be honest. You don't need to show anyone else.

5b. If you are working that day, don't worry about documenting how you spend your time there. Just state that you'll be at work.

4. State how you usually feel at this time of day as follows and don't overthink the response: Average, Less than Average, Better than Average.

5. State whether you typically consume alcohol/drugs at this time of day.

Afternoon
12:00 – 18:00:

1. State whether you usually have a break in the day for lunch.

1a. If so, state the full time you usually take that lunch break. E.g.: 1pm – 2pm.

1b. What you usually eat for lunch. E.g.: Sandwich, McDonalds, Salad.

2. If you usually do something with your time other than eating, state what this is. E.g.: I go for a walk, smoke a cigarette, read a book, etc.

3. State how you usually feel at this time of day: Average, Less than Average, Better than Average.

4. State whether you typically consume alcohol/drugs at this time of day.

Evening
18:00 – 02:00

1. If you're typically working on that day, state whether you're usually home from work by now. If not state the time you get home.

2. State the time you eat your evening meal on that day. If it's irregular and hard to estimate, note this.

2a. Give an example of a typical meal you would eat that evening. E.g.: Homemade pasta, Supermarket ready meal, Cheese on toast, etc.

3. State whether you attend any clubs, if so, the time including travel time and follow up time. For example, if you have a Yoga class and leave your house at 18.15, class is 18.30 – 19.30, travel home 19.30 – 19.45, sit down exhausted 19.45 – 20.15, shower and change 20.15 – 20.30.

You'd state Yoga 18:15 – 20:30.

4. Include any typical family/friend commitments. If you spend Thursday night with the parents or typically go out drinking 3 times a week, include it.

5. Include all other activities you regularly partake in.

6. State the time you usually go to bed. If it's irregular or hard to estimate, note this.

7. State how you usually feel at this time of day: Average, Less than Average, Better than Average.

8. State whether you typically consume alcohol/drugs at this time of day.

Once you're finished you should have something similar to the example on the next page. This is a typical example from a client I've worked with in their mid-twenties. Don't worry if your current week looks completely different, the point of this exercise is to show yourself what you're really up to and how you're spending your time. That gives us a baseline to work from and will stop us demanding too much from ourselves too soon.

This book will work best for you if you stop reading and complete the exercise now. Though of course, the choice is your own. Be sure to bookmark the page if you're planning to come back later.

OCCUPATION NAVIGATION

	Monday	Tuesday	Wednesday	Thursday	Friday	Saturday	Sunday
Morning	Wake up at 7.45am Usually shower Skip Breakfast Leave at 8.30, commute to work for 25 minutes. Feel less than av'ge. Social media 10mins. No drink/drugs.	Wake up at 8.00am Usually shower Skip Breakfast Leave at 8.30, commute to work for 25 minutes. Feel less than av'ge. Social media 10mins. No drink/drugs.	Wake up at 7.45am Usually shower Skip Breakfast Leave at 8.30, commute to work for 25 minutes. Feel less than av'ge. Social media 10mins. No drink/drugs.	Wake up at 8.15am Usually shower Skip Breakfast Leave at 8.30, commute to work for 25 minutes. Feel less than av'ge. Social media 10mins. No drink/drugs.	Wake up at 6.30am Usually shower Skip Breakfast Leave at 8.30, commute to work for 25 minutes. Feel less than av'ge. Social media 10mins. No drink/drugs.	Spent morning asleep, wake up around noon. No work today. Feel less than average.	Spend morning asleep, wake up around noon. No work today. Feel less than average.
Afternoon	Break 1.15-1.45pm Walk to supermarket and buy meal deal No drink/drugs. Feel average.	Break 1.00-1.15pm No time for lunch Feel less than average. No drink/drugs.	Break 1.00 - 2.00pm Go out to eat with colleagues, walk to regular bar. Typically eat a burger. Drink a gin and tonic. Feel better than average.	No break or lunch, might snack from vending machines in the afternoon. Feel less than average. No drink/drugs.	Leave work early on Fridays, don't take lunch. Sometimes I bring a sandwich to eat at my desk but usually not. Feel average. No drink/drugs.	Cook bacon and eggs around 1pm. Take a shower. Watch TV. Catch up on Social media. Do some laundry. Smoke a joint. Feel less than average.	Make a smoothie and eat toast around 1pm. Watch TV. Catch up on social media. Visit parents around 3pm-8pm. Feel less than average. No drink/drugs.
Evening	Home around 6pm. Eat around 9pm, maybe beans on toast? Kickboxing 6.15-8.30. Watch TV 9pm-11pm. Smoke a joint Drink a gin and tonic. Go to bed around 12.30am. Feel av'ge.	Home around 6pm Eat around 7pm, probably a ready meal or oven food. Go out with friends 8.30pm - 12.00am Drink a lot Go to bed around 1am. Feel average.	Home around 6pm. Take-away around 8pm. Usually speak to family on the phone. Sometimes go out but not every week. Smoke a joint. Watch TV. Go to bed around 11pm. Feel less than average.	Home around 6pm Eat around 7pm, probably a ready meal or oven food. Go out with friends 8.30pm - 12.00am Drink a lot Go to bed around 1am. Feel average.	Home around 4pm Go to the gym for two hours. Go out with friends to eat 7pm - 3.00am Drink a lot Go to bed around 4am. Feel average.	Eat instant noodles around 5pm. Watch some TV. Go out with my friends for drinks around 9pm. Get home at 2am, eat a kebab. Feel better than average.	Parents make some home cooked food. Get home around 8pm. Watch a film maybe. Smoke a joint. Spend a few hours on social media. Go to bed around 11pm. Feel better than average.

Excellent, congratulations on finishing the first step towards a better life! It might not seem like much, but you now hold in your hands the blueprint to how you're currently living your life. This is what you do on average every week of your life. Take a long hard look at this. It should be an honest reflection of exactly the type of person you are based on your current habits and behaviours.

Do you feel like the blueprint of your life is an honest reflection of who you are? Are you happy with how you're currently living and how you're spending your time? For almost everyone I've ever done this exercise with, the answer is no. They don't feel like the way they're currently living their lives reflects who they are or what they're capable of. Let's go through some key points to put all of this into context.

Firstly, let's remember back to when we spoke about the importance of having some genuine compassion for ourselves and our circumstances. For a lot of people having their lives laid out on display like this is an unwelcome awakening. They can see instantly lots of areas where they're going wrong and feel an immense desire to put everything right, right away. Worry not, remember we're working together to straighten things out here. We're going to set you on the path to success and a better life. To do that, you need to know who you are right now. You must face that person. You are what you do every day, and now you can see what you do every day. Are you the person you thought you were? I know I wasn't when I did this exercise for the first time. In truth the realisation levelled me. I was getting by on my moralistic good intentions and work ethic. I didn't enjoy stripping that away to see how I was actually manifesting myself in the world. However, I recognised this step as essential. Without it I would have remained blind and continued deceiving myself about how bad things really were.

By now you've likely realised what we mean by "there will be sacrifices" to achieve your ambitions. You're going to sacrifice things you enjoy doing that aren't helping you. You're going to sacrifice some of your wasted time for productive endeavours. You might even need to sacrifice spending time with some of the people in your life who are holding you back from reaching your potential. We need to set ourselves up properly before we can set out on our course for world domination. After all, how dare you try to look after a book of clients or a team of people when you can't even look after yourself. How do you expect people to take you seriously when you don't even respect yourself enough to look after yourself very well?

What exactly should we do to put things right? Start small. Start smaller than you'd like to. Humble yourself. Remember you are the Captain and must work with your crew to put things right. They don't want to start running marathons without any training and won't stand for it. They might help you fix things if properly incentivised though. Take a look at your life, the blueprint you've created. What's the smallest thing that you would be willing to change about it? I highly recommend starting by removing bad habits, rather than trying to form new ones. Below are some typical areas that might need your attention, and a strategy for dealing with them.

Do you get up at approximately the same time every morning? This does matter because your body regulates its functions using your circadian rhythm. The circadian rhythm is commonly observed in all living creatures. It's responsible for making sure your blood pressure increases before you naturally wake up so you're not still tired after a good night's sleep. It makes sure you secrete melatonin into your blood stream so you can fall asleep in the first place, and stops that secretion once you're awake. It impacts your hormone production. Amongst other issues this has a profound effect on mood and wellbeing, but we won't discuss the impacts of hormonal imbalances in men and women within this book. Your circadian rhythm is also the reason you experience jet lag while you adjust to new time zones, even if you're well rested. There are clear patterns of changes in core body temperature, hormone production, brain wave activity, cell regeneration, and so forth. In nature the light from the sun along with temperature fluctuations naturally keep the rhythm. As modern people, we are fully in control of our lighting and heating conditions under most circumstances. This is technologically a miracle. However, it can play havoc with our circadian rhythm and make it difficult for us to regulate the functions it controls, such as sleeping and waking. To make things easier for ourselves we can do a few things.

1. Start by waking up at the same time every morning. This is more important than the time you go to bed. Be realistic with this, pick a time you like and set an alarm.

2. Make sure your alarm clock isn't next to your bed. You do not have a great level of self-control the second you wake up, and it's too tempting to just snooze through. If you make yourself get out of bed to turn off your alarm clock, you'll have the discipline to stay out of bed.

3. Decide in advance what you're going to do the second after you've turned your alarm off. Make this the same every single morning. This can be whatever you like, but make it something simple that gets you outside your bedroom. Perhaps go and drink a glass of water or brush your teeth, shower or make a cup of tea. Something easy that gets you away from your bed. Don't try to build a full morning routine until you've mastered getting out of bed as soon as your alarm goes off. Do this for a full week before trying to change anything else.

4. Snoozing makes you more tired for the rest of the day. You will feel drowsier all day if you snooze for even 5 minutes. This is a bigger issue than you think if you're trying to build yourself into a success. You'll be competing against people who don't feel drowsy while they're working, and they might well outwork you. However, I get it, you'd think an extra few minutes would be a good

thing especially if you've under-slept. The problem is your body doesn't have enough time to get back into deep sleep, which is rejuvenating. Instead you simply mess with your body clock by confusing it with messages about what the alarm sounding actually means. You need to condition yourself to get out of bed when the alarm sounds. Give it a week, you'll find it far easier to wake up and feel less tired throughout the day.

5. Make your environment darker and cooler at least one hour before bed, this mimics a more natural environment we've evolved over millennia to deal with.

6. Blue light filters. The research indicates that the blue light emitted from our screens suppresses the production of melatonin, and as such can keep us awake. Install a blue light filtering application on your devices and use it after 6pm. Plenty are available from the app store or just online.

7. 3 Day Rule. It takes at least 3 days to establish a new sleeping pattern. In short, if you're currently going to bed at 1.30am every morning and start trying to go to bed at 11pm, you'll struggle to fall asleep at the new time for at least 3 days. This is fine, stick with it or preferably adopt a more gradual approach. Moving your bed time backwards by 15 minutes every few days. You're unlikely to shock your system this way. In brief you must make your sleeping pattern routine. Your body and mind will thank you for it.

Next, we're going to outline the true process for making the real changes necessary to form the right routines. You can then apply the changes needed to all things on your blueprint. Take a look at your original blueprint. What other areas could do with some improvement? Perhaps you're looking at your diet and exercise regimen (or lack of one), this is a good thing. These deserve some individual attention and will be addressed later in the Health 101 section of the book. For now, let's outline the mechanics of lasting change.

Here is a simple and effective key to success: write down what you're trying to achieve. Set yourself goals and bring them to life by writing them down. This will make you think clearly. We're going to continually revisit goal setting because it's so critical to your success. In the context of creating an effective routine, properly set goals will allow you to set a target and measure your progress towards it. This will clearly define the goal so you know when it's been achieved. The concept is simple and important. Define what you want, how you're going to do it, then take the steps that you've pre-defined as necessary to complete it. SMART goals are an excellent way of doing this because they give structure to the process and make us think carefully about what we're actually doing. They also prevent us from setting vague goals which cannot be achieved. "Clean up house" is a bad goal because it's unclear what success would look like, after all there's always something else which can be done when cleaning a house. "Wipe down the kitchen surfaces, hoover the kitchen floor and take out the bins as soon as I come home from work" is better because it defines what success looks like. When dealing with complicated goals, we can and should build on this further. That's where SMART goals come in. SMART is an acronym which stands for: Specific, Measurable, Achievable, Relevant, Timebound. Spending a moment to write your goals down in this format will massively increase your chances of actually executing them successfully. Remember, each time you achieve one of your goals, no matter how small, you're moving towards a better life. Let's go through the process of setting a smart goal together. Let's again suppose you're trying to form a better sleeping routine for this example, using the smart goal format.

Specific – Specify exactly what it is you're trying to achieve, the more detail the better.

Example: I want to establish a better sleeping routine. I will sleep at least 7 hours every single night, I also recognise the importance of waking up at the same time each morning and will work to achieve this.

Measurable – How will you measure your progress; how will you know exactly when you've been successful?

Example: I will measure my progress by writing down how well I've slept each night as soon as I wake up the following morning. I will know I've successfully achieved this goal when I've recorded a full week of waking up at the same time each morning with a full 7 hours of sleep.

Achievable – How exactly do you personally achieve this goal, what will you do to make it attainable?

Example: I will research the best ways to develop a healthy sleeping routine and apply this knowledge.

Relevant – How is this goal relevant to what you're doing with your life? What makes it worthwhile?

Example: This goal will help me be more productive at work and less tired throughout the day. Other benefits include allowing me to get more done with my mornings and regulate my circadian rhythms better, which will improve my mood and hormonal balance.

Timebound – How long are you going to give yourself to achieve this goal?

Example: I will start this goal next Monday, and have achieved the measurable success specified above within one month of my start date.

You can easily see how useful SMART goals are in moving you forward with direction. Use them as a tool to build a powerful daily routine. Fix the things that announce themselves to you personally as in need of attention. This will require some sacrifice. Perhaps you notice that your drinking is impacting your ability to keep a routine, you'll need to make your own decisions on whether or not to get this under control. If this applies to you and you're unwilling or unable to get this under control, you may have a serious problem and it is strongly recommended you seek outside help in this circumstance. You should still write down your goal even if you feel you need help to reach it. The process of writing the goal down means you're taking it seriously and are much more likely to take the actions needed to achieve it. In another case, perhaps you notice the time you're spending with your intimate partner is preventing you from looking after yourself properly. In this case you may need to restructure your relationship into something more productive. Whatever it is holding you back, it's unlikely to be easy to fix overnight with minimal effort. However, it is essential that you develop a routine that allows you to look after yourself and meet your responsibilities outside of work properly. Without this you'll be unable to compete with the people who have their lives in order. As with all things in life the further behind you are, the more work you'll need to do to get back on track. There is something noble and respectable about sorting yourself out, in the process you'll become the sort of person capable of sorting out much greater things. A person of value and utility to those around you. This is admirable, and the world needs more people like this.

You'll need somewhere to document and keep track of your new routine. This will allow you to see how you're now spending your time. It's also a source of great motivation and encouragement to compare your new routine to your original blueprint every few months and see how far you've come. Use something simple, most of us have google calendar (or similar) already installed on our smart phones. Use this to input the new routine you're forming. This will allow you to easily set the tasks to repeat everyday or every week as appropriate, and you can set notifications up to remind yourself as appropriate. As we've already discussed, don't take on too much at once. Importantly, don't be too hard on yourself for failing to hit your new goals with 100% accuracy all the time. We're all human, not machines. If you develop new routines and hit them with 30% accuracy, you're already doing a lot better than before. Keep aiming upwards. As you establish the right patterns and behaviours it will become far easier to stay on track. Consistency is your friend here. Keep noticing areas where you can improve and try to get better every week. Keep track of your progress and remember where you started.

Be sure to reward yourself when you reach your goal and when you achieve successes along the way. As captain, proper rewards and incentives are your greatest ally in keeping the crew on board. This might sound unnecessary but don't overlook the reality of your psychology. You're a person, and its human nature to want to be rewarded for your work. You wouldn't work for someone else for free. You wouldn't expect someone else to work for you for free. It's unwise to expect yourself to work for free. Be realistic about this and reward yourself fairly. Starting small, perhaps you allow yourself to have your favourite take-away on the nights you don't go out drinking. Perhaps you make a deal with your partner that if they'll support you in regaining control of your time, you'll spend some quality time with them on Saturday morning doing something interesting you both enjoy. As a rule of thumb, people will generally prefer a smaller amount of your undivided attention, in comparison to spending every second of the day with you while you're half distracted and concerned about other things.

A side note on relationships: You and your partner should want what's best for each other, but if you're the one making changes it is your responsibility to manifest this as something agreeable to both of you. Do not expect them to adapt straight away. After all, they're in love with the version of you they know right now and have likely grown to expect a level of predictability. If you suddenly start changing, especially if this is out of character for you, you can unsettle the other person. This is natural, you can give them time to adjust and help them see the positives for both of you.

Back to incentives and reward. These were just a couple of very specific examples of things you could do to reward yourself for your new healthy behaviours. Sit down and consult yourself on the things you might use to justify your own hard work, promise yourself these things and deliver them to yourself on completion of your set goal. Make the reward proportional to the goal. Don't book a five-star holiday to the Maldives for putting on a load of laundry, but maybe make yourself your favourite hot drink and watch a YouTube video if that's your thing.

Figure out how much reward it takes to incentivise yourself, everyone is different. This is a great way of getting to know yourself. You'll likely find the more you make things routine, the easier they are to do and the less reward you'll need to keep doing those things. The more routine things become, the less complicated and demanding they become on our resources. It's difficult to run a 5K race if you've never run before, but it's comparatively easy if you're a seasoned marathon runner.

Routines take time to establish and you won't be perfect right away. Stick at it. It's worth it. It will make your life easier and more manageable. This is essential to becoming the type of person you want to be. You cannot be truly happy without one. So, work hard to develop a good one. Do the exercises laid out in this chapter and make a commitment to sticking to your new way of life, observing and improving, for a minimum of 3 months. Done properly you'll set rock solid foundations upon which you can build the rest of your life high into the clouds.

Chapter 3
Vision

Congratulations on making it this far. By now you should be functioning well in the world and looking after yourself with compassion. That's not a trivial or easy thing to achieve. Getting this far means you're starting to treat yourself with the respect you deserve. As such, it's time to start demanding a bit better for yourself. We need to start thinking bigger.

We need to develop a compelling vision to work towards. It needs to be uniquely yours. We'll work through it together every step of the way. However, no abstract dreams of retirement at the age of 40 yet. We're keeping our feet firmly planted on the ground and starting small, because we've already learned that this is the way to achieve success. One step at a time. In this chapter we'll develop a compelling vision of you in 10 years, a slightly higher resolution vision of you in 5 years, and a crystal-clear image of yourself 12 months from now. We'll build an action plan complete with SMART goals to get you there. Rest assured, this section may be easier than you think. Developing a vision for your life is one of the most rewarding, highest return steps you can take on this journey. It requires no heavy lifting or gruelling work either. The more things you've already done with your life, the easier this will be. This is because the more experiences you've had, the more you've already learned about what you do and don't like. Particularly the things you don't like. This information is useful and will help us form our vision.

A vision is often compared to a star shining brightly in the sky at night. It's something beautiful. It helps you navigate when you're lost. You can clearly see if you're walking towards it or away from it. In setting out a vision for your life, you should be giving yourself something meaningful to work towards. Every single person who has ever been a success in life has had to overcome obstacles. You will face difficulties and tragedies on your way to the top. It's for this reason you must have a compelling vision for your life. It's common for people to be entirely derailed by difficult events in their lives and end up unconsciously walking down the wrong path. Often times there's chance associated with these occurrences and they may well be outside of our direct control. With a vision in mind of where you're heading, you'll be able to spot when you've been derailed and are heading in the wrong direction. Without one, you may end up a long way away from anything ideal and not realise until it's far too late.

You already have a vision of who you're meant to be. You know this. Every time you let yourself down by making decisions that are bad for you, you're actually letting down your idealised self. This is why you feel bad. You know what's good for you and what isn't already, and in the long term you don't feel good when you do things that aren't good for you. The guilt you feel when you're over-indulging in food is a message from your better self, telling you this isn't the path forward. The vision you already have of yourself probably isn't very clear, but it does exist. You could explain this from a theological or evolutionary perspective. Either way, this inarticulate vision of a better you is there to keep you alive and on the right path. The exciting thing is that you can consciously choose the path you're going to take in life. This might sound obvious, but few people actually do this. Instead opting for a safe journey without ever really waking up to their true potential. At least, not until it's far too late.

So then, a good start might be to consult yourself on when you feel like you're letting yourself down. Do you feel good about lying to people, eating too much, drinking too much? Do you feel good about having a messy living space? Not being recognised by others for your contributions? Being weak when people need you? Hurting vulnerable people? These questions are for you to answer. But by asking yourself these questions you can form a fairly good idea of who you are. Consult your resentments and emotions and try to verbalise the things you value. Don't feel good about lying or being lied to? Perhaps you value honesty and the truth. That's a good thing to know about yourself. It should also make you think twice about lying to people for power or status, or because you think you're trying to protect them from some truth they can't handle. If you value the truth (whether you like it or not) you'll never be truly happy or able to respect yourself unless you're honouring that value. You'll start to get serious about only keeping honest people around you. You'll realise one of the reasons you don't respect yourself is maybe because you feel the need to lie to people. If you don't respect yourself you won't look after yourself properly, and your life will have a tendency to fall apart for all the reasons we've already discussed.

Ask yourself these questions and more, really dig deep into the things you don't like about the world and other people in particular. Take money as an example. You'll likely find the question isn't as simple as "Do you value money?" Because that's not a very simple yes or no question. Instead, you'll need to consider the things money can be used for. A better question to ask yourself is "Is money something that would be valuable to me in achieving my ambitions to do good in life?". This is because we all know great achievements like sending mankind to the moon or curing smallpox take huge amounts of money. On the flip side of the coin terrible things like war take huge amounts of money. Don't get too idealistic in your thinking either, ask yourself these questions in the world you currently live in. Don't think money would be all good only if there was no war or if it wasn't used to create weapons of mass destruction. We live in a world where both of those things are a reality. Don't try to mess with reality. Because an honest answer may tell you that you respect people who use money for good, not bad. Therefore, one of your values is probably to have money but to ensure it's used for good. This might mean providing for your family and sending your children to university, and not spending it all on heroine (and thereby funding the cartels who produce it) or not investing in companies that fund child labour. Remember it's your life and your decision and I'm not here to tell you what to think. I'm here to help you figure out what you already value. Perhaps you value people with integrity and realise you expect the same from yourself. Same with dependability. Perhaps people who take on challenges inspire you, and you don't respect people who refuse to do this. This exercise is similar to the one we did before establishing how to change your daily routine. It will help us establish who you really are. It will help you understand what people mean when they tell you "Just be yourself". By the way, most people who give you that advice don't know what it means either. But you both know it's right somehow. This is why. Figure out who you are according to your values this way. Write down the answers. This will help you remember them, which will help you stay true to yourself, which will stop you growing resentful towards yourself and others. Remember you're basically looking for things that you either really don't like about other people, or really respect about them. This will tell you what you value. If you really get stuck, you can do a google search for personal values and try to figure out whether you expect them from yourself and others. If so, it's likely one of your values, even if you're not acting it out in the world right now. Make a list of your top values that you feel make up who you truly are most accurately. I.e.: without living your life according to this value, you know you'll be living a bad life that makes things worse for yourself and others. Narrow this list down to between 5 and 10 core values that are the most important to you personally. Once you've done this, we can work on figuring out what you want to do to make yourself a success. Without this step, you'll likely end up doing something that isn't true to who you are. That would be a true tragedy for you because you'll be unhappy and resentful, unable to respect yourself, and you won't know exactly why. It's a bad path to be on and since this is a book about success, it's an obligation to tell you how to avoid that path.

Once you have a list of five to ten values we can move forward. One of the reasons the previous exercise was so important is this. If you value the truth, common sense and personal integrity, you better be working in an environment that allows you to be who you are. If a manager or the like is expecting you to regularly lie, ignore your common sense and then to top it off, that manager has no integrity... the chances you'll enjoy working for such a person are practically zero. Equally if those values aren't core to who you are, you could probably tolerate such a manager for a period of time in order to do great work or secure a promotion, whatever your reasons may be. It's important to know these things about yourself. You're no good to anybody if you're bitter and resentful about putting up with your daily grind. It's a bad way to go through life, but you'll meet countless people who bend themselves out of shape for no good reason in low paying jobs for years. Usually because they can't see a better alternative. What a tragedy.

A note on growing up, no matter how old you are. Sometimes you're bitter and resentful because you're immature. Maybe someone senior to you at work has made an unnecessary change that effects your life negatively and makes it far less enjoyable for you to go to work. Perhaps you need to say something to someone in power, and you refuse to say it because you're scared. This is understandable. It is not an effective way to go through life. You'll notice the people you look up to and respect have the ability to say what needs to be said, when it needs to be said. They don't hide or sit on their resentment; they confront the perpetrator with bravery. Likewise, sometimes when people upset you it's because you have an inflated sense of entitlement or refuse to change. If that's true you need to shut up and stop complaining. Nobody likes a whiner. Everybody respects the brave. If you take a minute to consider these things carefully, you probably already know exactly what you need to do. If you're really not sure whether you're whining unnecessarily or if you're actually just avoiding your problems by being too afraid to speak; speak to someone you trust outside your company. A personal friend or loved one is usually best. Tell them impartially without trying to get them to agree with you on anything. They should tell you what they think. If you trust them, you should take their opinion into account. If you don't trust them, you shouldn't be telling them these things.

A small side note on finding someone to talk to. You won't find this included in personal development books from the past, but loneliness is now a serious epidemic in the western world. I hope this never applies to you. However, if your life is such right now (or ever in the future) that you have nobody you trust to talk to, you're in a dangerous place. I strongly recommend you consult a councillor at your earliest opportunity and have regular truthful conversations. Find a way to do this and do not let money or family or anything stop you. Your life will improve. Your life improving is the most valuable gift you can give to the world. It's noble and admirable to be the best person you can be and accept help along the way when needed.

With your list of five to ten core values in hand we can start to build a vision of you that is compelling and motivating. Picture yourself in ten years' time. You've been living up to your values the whole time. Now try to answer three questions:

1. Do you have a family around you? If not that's just fine.

- If you do, how many children do you have? Do you have a husband or wife? Then describe your standard of living. Upper middle class meaning the children all have their own bedrooms, they wear new fitted clothes and you can afford to buy them what they want for Christmas. Perhaps you can afford to take the whole family on holiday every year.

2. Are you living where you live now, or somewhere different?

If you live somewhere different, describe the type of home and location. Then use the internet to look up how much the particular home costs in today's money. E.g.: 5-bedroom town house in a large city, approx. £900,000. Or 2-bedroom flat in a small town, £150,000.

3. How much money are you earning? - Use the first two questions as a guide.

If you have 3 children and want to be living an upper middle class lifestyle in the UK (outside of London), you'll likely be earning at least £80,000 – if your partner also has an income.

What are the things you would like to do with your money? Nice car, invest for the future, beautiful home? Have fun with this part.

Great, we have a vision of you in ten years. Perhaps you're a woman with no children earning £150,000 a

47

year. You're living in a modest home and spend your money on expensive holidays and have a new Aston Martin in the driveway. Maybe you're investing so you can start a family soon. Perhaps you're a married man with 3 children earning £80,000. Covering all your expenses nicely and giving your children a good life. Perhaps you're a single woman with a child, earning £50,000 but living on your own terms in a beautiful area that doesn't cost a fortune. You can provide everything your child needs and have a fully flexible working schedule that lets you spend lots of time at home. Whatever the reality of your situation, figure out what it would take for you to be satisfied with your last ten years achievements. Remember this isn't the end goal of your whole life, this is 10 years from now. Think big here. The focus is to have a compelling vision of where you could be one short decade from now. This vision is deliberately low resolution and we'll work back from here on purpose. You do not need to specify your specific job title or revenue streams unless you already know these things with 100% accuracy.

The five-year vision. Things are starting to get serious now. By this point you should be half way towards your 10 year goal. You've put in the necessary work and laid the foundations for success ahead. You're working in the right industry at this point. You've built up some relevant experience and have some strong connections. So let's begin with this in mind. The first question is this;

what industry do you want to work in? That's a big question. Maybe you already know with conviction. If so excellent. However, if you don't, we'll do some thought experiments to work this out. We'll then need to figure out how to break into that industry at a level that will allow you to reach your 10-year goal. Here's the thing, you can earn good money in most industries. The catch is that you must be at the right level. Assuming you want to earn a reasonable amount of money in exchange for your efforts, there are a couple of areas we'll be ruling out straight away. Firstly, most customer facing high street retail positions are out. The possible exceptions being managers of large high street banks, at the time of writing this job can net you between £40,000 - £80,000. I'd argue this isn't the most effective way to earn a sizable wage in the financial services industry either, unless it's really what you want to be doing. Managers of large supermarkets can fall into the same category. Next on the list are administrative and telephony jobs for corporations. These can serve as excellent ways to enter large companies with career progression potential, particularly if you have limited experience or education. However, by the time you're 5 years into your plan, you'll need to be thinking bigger than this.

Here's something to consider. You'll often need to specialise and develop a specific skill in a certain valuable area to move up the career ladder. Once you've done this, you'll be able to demand a higher wage and generalise again. We're not going to get into the specifics of effective career planning yet, but this is important to know if you're trying to lay out an achievable vision for your life. Nobody pays big money for a jack of all trades and master of none, and this is usually very much what you are at the start of your career. Take 5 minutes to look at jobs commanding over £50,000 on your favourite jobs' website. You'll need a specialist skill. You're an excellent people manager, a computer programmer, project manager, Surveyor, Engineer, Web Developer, Auditor, Doctor, etc. You also need to think about whether or not your chosen profession or industry has a glass ceiling. This means, will you specialise in a field that pays you a high wage but doesn't have excellent career progression potential once you've specialised. A property surveyor may be a good example of this. You'll need to be willing to completely diversify later if this is your chosen path. For example, you could progress by becoming the manager of a team of surveyors, or maybe one day you may look to start you own firm. However, this will require an entirely new set of skills. Be aware of this at the outset. You will be investing large amounts of time and resources to reach your goal. You need to set out your 5-year vision with your 10-year vision in mind.

With all this in mind, choose a discipline to specialise in that closely matches your values and personality. If you have a very thick skin (you're comfortable with being disliked and challenged regularly), you're organised, and like developing the people around you, you might have what it takes to be a people manager. If you're an academic who places high value on reducing human suffering, perhaps your calling is to become a doctor. Technically minded and don't like putting up with politics and corporate bullshit? You'd make a great engineer, electrical, computing or otherwise. Technically minded and like working with people? Perhaps a web developer. Gifted with your hands and don't like to sit behind a desk? Welding and plumbing engineers make good money, keep in mind the glass ceiling we talked about earlier. Do people warm to you instantly and trust your opinions? You could make a lot of money in sales if you're in the right industry. Top tip, more senior sales agents are called "Relationship Managers" in most highly paid industries like financial services.

To help narrow down your choices, here are the top ten industries in the UK. I recommend immediately ruling out the ones with limited earning potential that will realistically prevent you reaching your 10 year vision or that do not match your values. If you're a hardcore environmentalist you'll probably want to avoid supporting the Oil and Gas industry for instance. Narrow the list down to your top 3, from there we can move into the desired position. Note most of these industries provide large and varied career progression routes and options. For instance, the transport and logistics category includes everything from lorry drivers to airline pilots. The oil and gas industry needs people to work on the rigs and people to engineer every part of them. Those are usually quite different jobs. The point here is that it's difficult to choose the "wrong" industry. You'll need to specialise in the beginning but will pick up transferable skills along the way. It's not an impossible challenge to change industry later down the line. The project manager for the construction company will be snapped up by the financial services industry if they're the right fit, and vice versa.

Top Ten UK Industries:

Financial Services – Banking, Insurance, Accountancy, etc. Don't think you need to be a math whiz to make it here. This industry employs around 7% of the UK's working population, through some 40,000 different businesses that specialise in financial services.

Information Technology – This industry is growing and supports all the others. Encompassing everything from IT support and web development to designing and building the latest computer hardware. If you're young and have the slightest interest in this industry, it's worth exploring further. The trouble is that as this is a constantly evolving field, a lot of the jobs you'll ultimately be in the market for don't exist yet. You'll need to be adaptable, however, the rewards are great. Currently employing around 3.7% of the UK population, this is a large growing industry.

Construction – This industry is huge, employing nearly 10% of the UK's working population. There are around 280,000 construction businesses in the country. It's no secret the UK has had a house building shortage for decades which has helped to make UK private property some of the most expensive and highly valued in the world. When it comes to this, don't just think construction labourers. Most trades and a large proportion of engineering professions are utilised here. These professions have more earning potential than they're given credit for. As over 50% of the population are earning university level educations, trades people will often out-earn their university educated counterparts as their skills and labour become rarer and more sought after. Do not dismiss this career path if you're a practically minded person with an aptitude for problem solving. If you do attend university to become a technical engineer in any field, you'll also be highly valuable. The STEM fields (Science, Technology, Engineering and Mathematics) are undersubscribed and the demand for people with these skills is great. Construction also encompasses architects, project managers and a myriad of other professions. A great industry for any young professional.

Oil and Gas – This industry is predicted to grow in size over the next two decades. This may seem surprising given the drive towards renewable energy, but it continues to provide solid employment options for talented people in many areas. Oil rig workers are some of the highest paid labourers. The industry is investing heavily in renewables and is well known to invest in the education of its employees. If you've ever wanted to live in Scotland, 45% of total UK jobs in this sector are located there.

Government – This is a meta-sector that encompasses most of the healthcare and education industry in the UK. This also includes the military. It should be noted public administration, along with local and central government support are large in their own right. The civil service is a large sector that helps the government of the day implement its policies. Paying benefits and pensions, running prisons, issuing driving licences, etc. You may find this line of work rigid, although efforts have been made in recent years to innovate. Wages can also be very reasonable in exchange for the demands of the work. Carefully investigate the progression potential in your line of work here, but this can be a great option for some people.

Healthcare – Doctors, Nurses, Scientists, Dentists, Pharmacists, Psychologists, Care Home Management. The high paying options here are rewarding and varied. Some 12% of the population are employed in healthcare related fields. Huge demand and underfunding of these services actually drives up their value. You'll often need a higher education to enter this field, but your return on investment should make this field appealing and lucrative. We'll talk about why it may be worth retraining for the right career later.

Manufacturing – Since the industrial revolution the UK has had a rich tradition of manufacturing. Something that continues today in the modern era as the industry employs some 12% of the working population. This industry has had to adapt to survive. Think consumables like food, beverages, tobacco, as well as the more well-known electronics, cars and components for everything we use. Engineers, technicians, purchasing managers and the like are strong options in this field.

Wholesale and Retail – This is one you want to be on the right side of. Shop floors and even management positions are generally out. The notable exceptions already discussed. To make any serious money here you'll need to be based out of a head office or running multiple customer facing sites. Still, this is one of the easiest industries to break into with limited education and experience and there's something to be said for that. The industry is one of the largest too, although most positions are the ones we already know to approach with caution.

Transport and Logistics – Technological innovation (think Uber for taxi drivers) is reshaping this industry fast. With multiple companies working to automate the jobs associated with the transports of goods and people, the big money is in working with the large corporates on these technological advancements.

Education – Increases in university places and fees in recent years has led to a corresponding increase in faculty staff and administrative support. If you're a born academic this will be your calling. Don't fall into the wrong position without a plan, statistically you'll be a primary school teacher for a long time before you find a promotion. Primary school teachers are essential to our way of life and deserve respect. However, if your 10 year vision is to be earning £150,000 this is a non-starter. This industry will require a clear plan for your success. Actual planning is something we'll move onto soon. For now, we're just looking at the major employment options.

So there we have the top 10 industries by GDP contribution and number of employees in the UK. Narrow these down to your top 3, doing some additional research if you feel this would help. I strongly recommend you make your choice based on your values. All these industries will offer you the potential to earn a good living. Once you've got your top 3, it's time to start thinking about what kind of position you'd like to be in 5 years from now. There's a couple of questions you should be asking yourself. Are you willing to obtain further qualification and/or education? I'd suggest this would be a wise decision if you've concluded you're on the wrong path in life right now. It won't be for everyone, but it will be worth if for those that specify a goal and are willing to work towards it. Human history has taught us much about success, and one of the key lessons to keep in mind is that successful people delay gratification. They're willing to go without today, so that they can have more tomorrow. This doesn't necessarily mean going back to school, it might mean taking a course in project management at your own expense to enter the field. It might mean reaching out to a career coaching expert who can help you break into your chosen field. Whatever the case, be willing to invest in yourself by sacrificing some of your current time and money and exchange for a better future.

Refusing to do so will drastically limit your options and will likely prevent you from moving forward. To help narrow down your options when it comes to positions, do some research. You can start with a simple google search for "The highest paid jobs in [insert industry name here]" or "50k jobs in [insert industry name here]". Jobs websites are your friend here. Once you've shortlisted 10 potential jobs across your top 3 industries, you have something tangible to work with. Write these jobs down on a sheet of paper. Get your values list out. Get your 10 year goals out. Rank order the jobs in order of how closely they match who you are (values) and what you want (10 year goals). When you do this, make a commitment to aim for the position that most closely matches both. You'll likely end up with a couple of different options that closely meet your criteria. You'll have to make a tough decision at this point. The truth is, whichever option you choose will be right. Be ambitious, choose the one that interests you the most or otherwise stands out in some way. We're going to drill down into the viability of the options in the career planning chapter. You might not be able to pursue your first choice for a variety of reasons but do not let that stop you now.

The important thing is to pick something. It should be something compelling, but you don't have to be completely in love with it. There's a lot of misinformation in the media. Particularly social media. Not being completely in love with your job for a short time to reach higher goals and develop yourself into a wealthy, intelligent person with a firm understanding of the way the real-world works (the world most people live in) is admirable and worthwhile. This goes against the advice you'll received from some popular social media influencers who advocate living your dreams at all costs. Here's something, it usually takes money and skills to live your dreams. If you're a young person, the chances you have an abundance of either are relatively low. What exactly does living *your* dreams actually mean anyway? You're in no position to start living on a beach in Bali running your ecommerce business selling fidget spinners... but if that's really *your* dream then you'll find 100 people willing to sell you a course on how to do that for a few thousand pounds. Before you buy into that ask yourself whether that person makes their primary income selling courses. Are they using advertising analytics to target young people? How much money (if any) they've ever even made themselves selling fidget spinners, or energy drinks, or makeup, or whatever it is. In reality *your* vision will shift as you begin working towards it, so you're not deciding your whole life right now. You'll have every opportunity to build any life you want. However, build yourself into someone with the expertise and knowledge to do that first. In the immortal words of Conor McGregor: "There's no secret sauce to this. Recognise what you need to do and fuckin' do it... you will succeed." Careers are valuable things which teach us a million lessons and if we master them, make us wealthy and give us status and place in the world. That's something admirable.

So, I'll say it again, you don't have to love your job. In the same way you don't love every second of school, or being a parent, or looking after your pets, or doing anything meaningful or worthwhile in life. We're not aiming at you being happy every second of the day here, that's too hedonistic and will take you down a path of self-destruction. The pursuit of pleasure over all else is no way to live your life. It will lead to you rejecting all responsibility. The meaning in your life will be found by adopting responsibility. You know this if you've ever worked hard to achieve something and done it. You know this if you've ever helped someone who genuinely needed it. You know this if you have a pet you love. You know this if you have children you love. If something is missing in your life and no tragedy is currently befalling you, you're likely missing the rewards associated with living a meaningful life. Great meaning can be found by taking your place in the world and doing great work. The most effective way to do this as a young person is through a meaningful career. Remember where you want to be in 10 years. That isn't going to happen by magic.

Key learning point: You are paid in accordance to the value society (the people around you) perceive that you provide to everybody else.

Schools are terrible at explaining this fundamental truth. This is basic economics, something poorly understood by those who have not worked in the free economy or studied the subject. Teachers in schools have typically never worked outside of the education machine in any meaningful way. Going from school to school (college) to school (university) and back to school. They have a specialist role in a state funded institution that isn't affected by the free markets in the same way. All your local high street shops could close, but your local school would stay open. School teachers are exceptional people who deserve respect and admiration. School teachers are also just as flawed as the rest of us and this point is something that no individual school teacher is ever placed with the responsibility of explaining to the younger generations. I make this point only because it's a tragedy.

Every time you hear someone complaining that they don't earn enough money, it's because they don't understand this point. You don't earn much as a retail shop assistant, or answering phones, or on a reception desk because your perceived overall individual contribution to everyone else is low and easily replaceable. If it usually takes a lot of you to keep things running, or if you individually quit tomorrow your organisation would not earn any less money, you're likely in a job that society perceives as low value. Your job might be incredibly difficult and worthy of respect. You will never be paid based on how difficult you find your job or how much respect you think you deserve. If your company would lose a lot of money, fall apart or people would die if you quit tomorrow, you'll be paid enough to make you stay. Great Doctors, Engineers and Commercial Airline Pilots are highly valuable people who are difficult to replace, and society places a high value on these people. You are paid in accordance to the value society (the people around you) perceive that you provide to everybody else.

So, pick a path that appeals to you that allows you to make the money you want. Specify a job position you want to have in 5 years and which industry you want to work in. It's not forever, it's to move you closer to your 10 year goal. It's to allow you to develop into the best person you could be, in accordance with your own values. You'll get plenty of happiness and positive emotion along the way if you stay true to yourself, now that you actually know what that means. Don't worry about exactly how you're going to get there yet. Pick something ambitious that would put you roughly halfway towards achieving your 10 year image of yourself.

Chapter 4
Career Planning

In this chapter we'll discuss how to make your vision a reality. You want to be the type of person who makes things happen. To do this we'll need an effective plan. For our purposes; we'll map out our approximate route to reach our 5 year goal, then map the next 12 months of your life in detail. This is a key move. We'll revisit this 12 month plan every year and rewrite it until we reach our 5 year goal.

Roughly mapping out your 5 year plan first will allow you to accurately identify your strengths and weaknesses against the job you want. This is crucial because it will tell you where you need to develop to get the position you want. In most circumstances this is ample time to increase your skills to get the job. If the challenge of increasing your skills is too great to achieve within 5 years, we've got two options. We can extend the timeframe for your dream job, or simply revisit your jobs list from earlier and realign your vision to your medium-term prospects.

For arguments sake, let's suggest as your first choice you want to work in the Transportation and Logistics industry. You recognise people and goods will always need to get places. You're also someone who values bravery and adventure, you don't like office politics but you're not entirely disagreeable either, you're somewhat above average in intelligence. Currently you're an able-bodied person with no excessively debilitating medical conditions. Your 10 year goal is to be earning £100,000 a year and travel the world. You've shortlisted your options and you decide it would be a great fit to become an airline pilot. Your other options in the top 3 are: Working in the Military to become an Officer in the Royal Marines or working in the Oil and Gas Industry as a Commercial Diver. Footnote: We've deliberately chosen specific niche jobs that won't apply to everyone, which is exactly what you should do.

Firstly, well done for getting this far. You now have a better understanding of yourself and your direction in life than 90% of your peers. With this knowledge we can build your life effectively. Remember the work we did to establish healthy routines? That's going to come in handy next. You need to be an effective person in the world to reach your goals. Living this way will also allow you to see things you would otherwise be blind to. Success is all about recognising what you need to do to get where you need to be, then doing those things. Career planning is no different.

So how do you recognise what you need to do? Your 5 year vision will light the path forward. Once you know what you need to do, there are actually a lot of people in the world who have a vested interest in helping you achieve it. Airline companies need pilots, the military needs generals, projects need managers, a university needs its students to stay open, etc. Understand that all companies, governments and institutions make a huge amount of money from you being successful. It's just not true that the system is set up against you and wants to see you fail. Even from a purely economic standpoint: better you do, the more money you earn your organisation, the more tax you pay. Everyone wants you to do well. True, you've probably encountered some selfish arseholes along the way who will get their kicks from putting you down. If somehow you haven't yet, you will. These people are the exception however, not the rule. By enlarge, almost all truly successful people want you to succeed. Anyone who doesn't will eventually go the way of dinosaurs with their failure to adapt and embrace new times. We'll deal with managing professional relationships later in the book. For now just remember, when you succeed things get better for everyone, so everyone who recognises this wants you to succeed. Truly successful people are smart enough to recognise this.

For this reason, there are endless resources in the public domain that will help guide you towards any particular career route you have in mind. A great resource for UK readers is the government website nationalcareers.service.gov.uk. You search for your chosen job and it will tell you which qualifications you'll likely need, along with the typical paths taken to get that job. Google is another invaluable resource, a simple "how to become a [insert job title here]" search and a couple of hours investigation will give you a lot of the answers you need. You just have to know what you want - which you now do. Regardless of how obscure the profession, there are resources out there. If there aren't many people who have made any money in your career field, comparative to the number of people pursuing it, the resources for guiding you will be limited. A search for "how to become a pop star" isn't fruitful because only 1% of the people who go down that route ever make serious money. Also, that particular career route usually involves being wealthy, knowing several successful music producers, having endorsement from other successful people, producing a body of work and writing a pitch that convinces a record company to invest around three million into your potential future success and marketing without any proven track record, and most importantly being very young and attractive or distinctive (body enhancements and facial tattoos are a good start). Being a great singer and song writer is usually optional. This just isn't something any successful person wants to be seen publicly advising people. There are exceptions to this "how to become a pop star" narrative; we all love a rags to riches story or someone willing to risk their reputation on a reality TV singing contest, or both together. In any case, lack of resources for the job you're investigating indicates you're looking into something shady likely run by a small network of people with a market monopoly. It's likely very few people make any money doing what you're looking to do. This isn't always the case, especially if the job you want is very new and has only just been created in the last 12 months. But proceed with caution here.

Alright so let's continue with the Airline Pilot example mentioned earlier. 20 minutes online gives you the basic formula. You're going to need a university degree in air transport/aviation and commercial pilot training. You'll also need a class 1 medical certificate. Once you've got the education, you'll be able to obtain a 'frozen' Air Transport Pilot Licence. You'll then need to work as a co-pilot/1st officer to build up the necessary experience to become an airline captain. This is an achievable and realistic goal. It also isn't the only option to become a pilot, but you've done your research and decide this is the most achievable option for you.

Nobody will spoon feed you everything you need, and you're going to need to make some sacrifices and take a measured amount of risk to pursue this path. Now you have your vision and an idea of what needs to happen. Let's turn this into a rough 5 year plan and exact 12 month plan as mentioned earlier. We'll then run an analysis of your current situation and skills to see if this path is something you can effectively pursue. All of this is critical to discover whether your plan is viable.

Alright so you need your degree and commercial pilot training. First thing, do you already have a degree? If you do, contact some airlines to see if they'll consider you with your current level of education. The trouble with this is that you'll be competing against people who have a degree in the right field. Unless there's a shortage of pilots you'll likely find that you need the air transport degree. Ok great, so you can chalk up the fees and time involved. Let's say 3 years and £45,000 for a standard degree. Next, you'll need the commercial pilot training. Many universities will include this with the degree, but it'll cost you an additional £80,000 - £120,000. You can do the training yourself separately for between £50,000 and £60,000. And it will take at least 2 years on average. So let's say you're looking at £100,000 in costs and at least 3 years of your life to qualify for your frozen licence and get hired by an airline as a 1st officer. Don't worry about the money yet. How long does it take to become an Air Captain once you're through the door? It largely depends on the airline and the economy. Somewhere between 18 months and 15 years. This will likely be the deal breaker in your plans. Let's say it takes you 2 years to become a captain once you've completed your degree and training. To invest £100,000 and then start earning £100,000 p/a within 5 years (3 years education/training,

2 years as a 1st officer) is a justifiable decision. To invest £100,000 and earn £25,000 a year as a 1st officer for the next 15 years is bad economics and will likely cripple your finances and keep you in a prison of debt. Unless you're exceptionally wealthy already and have no interest in return on investment, this is simply a bad investment of time and money. With this in mind, you may decide to pursue a lower investment, higher return career in the short term. Let's say you're currently not wealthy or even have existing debt. Once you reach your 10 year goal you can always finance the training yourself if you still want to be a pilot. Keep in mind you only just decided to investigate this vision and shouldn't be too attached to it. The choice of whether to go forward will be yours. Let's suppose you decide this dream is unobtainable for you in your current circumstances.

Personal analysis of strengths and weaknesses. We've already explored the power of self-knowledge as a life changing force. So far we've used it to improve our routines and develop a vision for our lives. Now we're using it to plan out our career. An honest analysis of our strengths and weaknesses will help making an appropriate career choice easier. Some people neglect this because it doesn't come intuitively, or perhaps because it can be a little uncomfortable to list our own weaknesses, but it serves the purpose of allowing us to choose a career that is best suited to who we are right now, in our current circumstances. It will highlight the path of least resistance towards your goals. You'll want to set aside 15 minutes to complete the exercise.

First, draw a chart like the one on the following page. Then add the necessary information to the relevant sections. The more time and detail you put into the chart, the more useful it will be. You'll then use this chart, along with your personal values and 10-year goals to decide which of your 5-year options is worth pursuing. With this in mind let's move forward.

In our example, you look at your strengths and weaknesses and realise that due to your existing debt and university education, you'll struggle to get the funding to retrain as an airline pilot. You'll need to self-fund this and cannot afford it. You don't know anyone who will give you the money, and you feel deep down that the risk is too high to justify at this point in your life. The possibility of becoming stuck for many years at the 1st officer stage and being indebted makes this unjustifiable. You've ruled out becoming a commercial airline pilot for now.

Your next choice was to become an officer in the royal marines. You recognise this path may be physically harder, but perhaps more rewarding in proportion. You've already made a commitment to live true to your values of bravery and adventure so decide this is worth exploring. You spend some time looking into the entry requirements and your career path, comparing what's needed to your strengths and weaknesses and identifying what you need to do next. You can see none of your current circumstances make this unobtainable and it's worth pursuing. You order your approximate career route as follows.

Application, interviews, successful induction to training may take up to a year. After this you'll enter basic training. That takes 15 months as an officer in the Royal marines. Unlike a university education or other training, you'll be paid to attend this from day one. You'll start off earning £26,000 a year, this appeals to you. After two years you'll earn a promotion to Captain. You're probably 4 years into your journey by now. You work out your approximate salary after 5 years is around £45,000 with all your living expenses covered (package value more like £60,000).

You decide all of this is agreeable and takes you towards your 10 year goal. You recognise the military will give you everything you could need to build a successful life. So you decide to aim for this. Now that you know it's possible if you apply yourself, you commit to working to make this a reality. You plan out the next 12 months of your life to make this a reality, working on the weaknesses you've already identified that might prevent you reaching your goal.

The process here is simple. Do your research so you recognise all the steps that need to be completed to achieve your goal. Writing a SMART goal (as previously discussed) can be very useful in helping you to identify the steps you'll need to take here. Spend at least 7 hours, or a full working day, researching and writing your plan for success over the next 12 months. After all, you'll be referring to this as your personal bible, it will literally tell you how to live your life over the next year. You want to get it right. Once you've recognised the steps you need to take, you should map these against each of the next 12 months. Use a format that works for you. No secret formula here. Just keep it as brief as you can. Use bullet points and short sentences. You want to be able to see it at a glance on a single sheet of paper. The path into the military is relatively simple, but the example is provided below for illustration purposes.

Month 1 – Make the necessary enquiries and submit your application to military. Start training to increase your fitness. You look up a military style training routine online and start doing this 2 days a week. It hurts at first, but you know it's important. You keep your current employment up for now.

Month 2 – You receive a letter back inviting you to an assessment centre and interview in two months' time. You increase the intensity of your fitness routine. It's getting easier now.

Month 3 – You keep increasing your fitness routine. You do all the research possible to give yourself a chance at passing the interview. You find out exactly what they're looking for. You start rehearsing what you're going to say in the interview section.

Month 4 – You complete the assessment centre. You receive a letter a week later to tell you that you've been successful. All the preparation paid off. You tell all your friends and family. They're proud of you. Your induction into basic training will happen in 3 months.

Months 5 – 7 – You keep training physically. You give notice to your current employer. You make the changes you need to make in your current life to join the military.

Month 8 – 12+ – Basic training time. This is what you've been preparing for. You give it everything you have. You realise you'll be here for the next 15 months. Your life is totally different now. All you have to do is stick with the programme and stay strong. You know you can do it. You think back to where you were a year ago and smile.

Use this structure regardless of your new chosen career path. You'll want a 12 month overview to keep you on track and progressing towards your newfound goal. The purpose of this monthly overview is to know whether or not you're on track or falling behind. It's hard to see this without having it clearly documented. Review this document regularly and hold yourself accountable. Rewrite the document at least every 12 months, or sooner if your plans change. Make sure the plan you make is true to yourself and your 10 year vision. If your next step doesn't fit into your longer term plans, reconsider it. Most people won't join the military because it won't be the right fit.

Have the courage to pursue your goals even if they're challenging and push you out of your comfort zone, behind that discomfort and unknown frontier is where some of the most rewarding parts of life are hiding.

Chapter 5

Gaining an Edge

If you've made it this far, you've successfully mastered the basics. You're ahead of the vast majority of the population already. Congratulations. You're on the road to a better life. The next problem you'll face is competing with the others at the top of their game. Competition is fierce up here. Nobody is going to graciously roll over and give you everything you want; you'll need to fight for it. Position, Status, Promotion. All areas of competition. The good news is that most of our western world functions more or less as a meritocracy. Meaning if you're the best, you'll usually win. It's not quite that simple, and there's plenty of nuance to muddy the waters. However, the simple truth is that you'll need to keep developing yourself if you want to reach your vision of who you could be. In the coming chapters we'll discuss the tangible skills you'll need. Interviews, negotiation, relationship management, looking after your health, and your increasing wealth - along with all the other tangible skills that go along with making yourself a success.

To start, we'll discuss the foundations of gaining an edge on your competition. It can be summed up in two words: Personal Development. In an ideal world, you'd be the best person you could possibly be. As you improve, your vision, capabilities and skills will also improve. This will lead to an increase in what you're capable of and move the vision of "the best person you could possibly be" to a continually higher level. This is a good thing. You already know this is true. Think back to who you were 10 years ago, are you the same person? Do you skill think the same way and make the same life choices? If you do, you have a lot of work to do. Chances are that you look back on your past self as a sort of less informed you more prone to making poor decisions. You develop, whether consciously or not. What personal development allows you to do is have more control over the person future you will become.

That's all well and good but where should you start? It seems likely you've picked up the first trick already. Read. Read a lot. Read books. Read articles. Read into things that interest you. Non-fiction. Great works of literature. Minus points for celebrity gossip magazines and click-baiting social media articles. When asked to self-report how many books they read a year, the typical person said they read 4. In contrast, 85% of millionaires read at least 24 books per year. This isn't a coincidence. Reading increases your knowledge of the way the world works. Reading increases your vocabulary. Reading increases your ability to communicate effectively. Of the 4 books the typical person reads each year, the vast majority of those are fiction novels. Fiction novels have their place, but as a reader of non-fiction books like this one, you already recognise their place in personal development. Difficult great works of fiction are also essential reading for anyone serious about becoming the best they can be. These stories contain universal truths about the world, other people in it, and your relationship to both of these things as an individual.

We're all limited creatures; we only have so much time, energy and resource. There's not enough of us individually to figure everything out on our own. Some things are best not learnt on our own anyhow. The proverbial touching of the hot stove not being necessary if someone pre-warns you that you'll get burnt. That's a lesson best learnt from someone else who has already touched the stove and experienced the pain. For eons our ancestors have been touching the hot stove so that we don't have to. Don't ignore their sacrifice for you. There's a reason you know not to jump off tall things, or go around aggressively shouting at strangers, or fist fighting large wild animals. These things may seem comically obvious. The truth is that all of your ancestors with a tendency to do these things died. The ones who didn't observed and survived.

Today, survival is much less about avoiding poisonous berries in the woods and much more about adapting and thriving in the modern industrialised world. Knowing not to eat the poisonous berries might be equivalent to knowing not to upstage your boss. The threats you'll face today probably won't kill you in a physical sense, they'll kill your chances of prospering. They'll keep you held down in the lower rungs of society. They'll keep you toiling away. Of course, some things will still kill you, perhaps you're yet to fully internalise the implications of excessive processed foods, cigarettes or alcohol. This is especially popular amongst young people. Perhaps because you won't find many people over 50 who are still sustaining a lifestyle of instant noodles, take-aways, heavy drinking and cigarettes. The ones who have made it to 50 with this lifestyle are suffering from several debilitating health conditions. Perhaps it's just because most people learn as they grow older. The point is this, knowledge is power. You don't have the time or resources to learn every lesson yourself. You're of course welcome to try. If you "die" trying, literally or figuratively, other people can learn from you. However, you probably have a higher calling in life than being a statistic for unemployment, divorce or cancer deaths.

Don't try to learn everything yourself. This is where books come in. Expand your mind with the knowledge from another mind. Read things from other people. Two brains are better than one. When you read someone's book, they're lending you their knowledge and brain power. Usually for a nominal cost. Books are incredibly cheap in today's world. Thank the powers that be for that. Further evidence that the system isn't against you.

If two brains are better than one, imagine the power of learning from 100 minds over the next few years, or thousands over your lifetime.

If you don't have time to read, ask yourself how anyone has time to read. After all, everyone has the same number of hours in the day. That's something we all have in common. How does the typical millionaire have time to read 24+ books every year? Surely they're busy working in their highly demanding careers or running big companies where people are depending on them. They have families, partners, commitments. It's because they recognise the limitations of themselves. They don't want to learn every lesson for themselves, that's far more costly and time consuming than learning from others. Successful people recognise the limitations of their individual being.

Make a commitment to read a certain amount over the next 12 months. A top tip is that audiobooks are great for fitting around your other commitments. Driving, on the train, cleaning the house, getting ready in the morning – audiobooks. Your mundane activity time just became valuable reading time. Successful people understand you don't have to block out 2 hours in the evening to learn things, you can fit it around your existing lifestyle with enough ingenuity. You'll find a lot of people (especially if they don't read much) think that audiobooks are a sort of cheating. You'll find people who "just prefer" the feel of an actual book. You'll find a bunch of other reasons people reject change and new technology. Leave these people to it. You'll be absorbing more information and reading more books.

How should you structure your reading, and how do you know what sort of reading commitment to make over the next 12 months? Let's break it down with some simple math. The average book is between 50,000 and 100,000 words. The average reading speed for an adult is between 200-400 words per minute. Imagine you're right in the middle of both of those statistics. You'll be able to read an average book with full concentration in a little over 4 hours. The key here is "full concentration", it's difficult to stay highly focused on anything for 4 hours. It can be done. However, let's say that you're a normal person who will take breaks, check your phone, look around and go to the toilet every now and again. Let's say you can read at 50% of full concentration with all this in mind. This would mean the average book will take you around 8 hours to complete. Fair enough. That's still not so bad. Imagine you commit to reading 12 books over the next year. That's 1 book a month. What exactly would you need to do to make that happen? You'd need to set aside just over 15 minutes a day of reading at 50% concentration. Or around 8 minutes a day of reading at full concentration. Don't listen to people who tell you that they don't have time to read. Get serious and plan those minutes into your schedule. Use audiobooks to read on the go, while you're commuting, cleaning up or doing any of your daily tasks that don't require much of your brain power.

Next up, getting around the right kind of people. Like-minded, supportive people. The type of people who make things happen, give you opportunities and want to see you succeed. Where do you find these people? The first trick is to be the sort of person you want to be around. Joe Rogan suggests to "Treat everyone as if it's you living another life". Timeless great advice. You'll start to attract the right kind of attention from the right people. You'll also attract some of the wrong kind of attention from people who think you're a benevolent soft touch, and it's your responsibility to reject those people so they're forced to become better people. Not because you want to hurt them back, but because you recognise it's not virtuous to be taken advantage of. If you allow people to take advantage of you, you're enabling their behaviour and allowing bad people to hone their skills. By rejecting these people from your life, you're helping them see the path upwards by showing them successful good people will not associate with them. That's not to say it's always the victim's fault if they're taken advantage of, but if you recognise this and have the power to stop it, you must do so. It protects the people who cannot do so.

Let's imagine you have a friend who always asks you for money, they desperately need it to get home or buy food for their cat or some other emergency. You oblige once or twice as a good friend. You start to notice that after your kindness, that "friend" starts to have regular emergencies they're unable to deal with themselves. You must ask yourself a question, are you enabling them to neglect their responsibilities to themselves and those around them by continuing to give them money? Is it *your* responsibility if *their* cat goes hungry? Or are you preventing the person from working hard enough to feed their own cat by bank rolling a "Get out of jail free" card for them. Is this person using their suffering and martyrdom to leverage your attention, money and sympathy on a continual basis? It is not virtuous to be taken advantage of by other people. Even if you feel like you're helping them and perhaps they'd just die without you. How did you allow another human being to hold you captive like this? Perhaps you have an unspoken agreement where you get to feel like a good person, and they get to leverage your time and resources in exchange. Consult your conscience for any troubled resentment in these circumstances, you'll know whether you're doing the right thing (or not) from how at peace you feel with yourself and your actions.

Bad people included, it's hard to argue against Rogan's reasoning. If we treated each other as if it were ourselves living another life, the world would be a better place. We can expand on this slightly to include some thinking from Immanuel Kant. In brief - act in a way that if everyone were to do it, it would be alright. These ideas together give us a decent foundation of morality with which to interpret the world. If these are the only two ideas you can articulate when someone asks you "How do you live a good life?" you'll be doing pretty well. They're included here for the same reason everything else is included, because you'll need them to be successful. Specifically, you'll need them to surround yourself with good people who want the best for you, which is an essential part of success.

One of the best ways to find the right kind of people is to attend seminars and events aimed at people like you. Half the value of these events is in the people you meet there, not just in the speakers who attend. You should also find ways to associate with senior people in your organisation or further afield, preferably who are doing things in the space you want to be in. More on exactly how to make those connections in the mentoring section. You can join clubs and associations that align to your vision and values. Do any charities or trusts do meaningful work that interests you? Chances are by helping them you'll meet the right kinds of people with similar interests. You'll also be able to present social proof that you are the type of person you claim you are, by virtue of you helping that charity or trust. Could you be the sort of person who gets a few tickets to the local fundraiser and invites a few of your trusted family and friends? Again, this will put you in the right circles. The trick is usually to minimise your exposure to events where alcohol or drugs are the main reason for the gathering. There's nothing morally wrong with these events or the people who attend, and there's a time and a place. Being reasonable tells you that if the alcohol is the main reason for the gathering and people's values and visions come a distant second or third place, it might be more difficult to find people who want the best for you. You're more likely to find people who just want a good time.

It's important to surround yourself with great people who want the best for you. The late great Jim Rohn said, "You are the average of the five people you spend the most time with". This is close enough to the truth to be carefully considered. Have you ever found yourself associating with people who didn't want the best for themselves? What happened when you were associating with these people? You'll understand this intuitively if you've had phases where you've spent too much time going out late nights with friends, or online gaming excessively, or perhaps a friend you met through smoking. You and your pals all start reinforcing your self-destructive behaviours. Not cool. You don't want to be the average of these people. This could be holding you back more than anything else. Social obligations to people who don't want the best for you or themselves. Lead by example here. Sort yourself out and aim upwards. They'll either be inspired and follow your example or try to pull you back down to your old ways. This is a good way to tell if people are really your friends, or if they just like a version of you that allows them to act badly and feel supported in doing so. Remember the sacrifices we discussed as necessary to your success? Leaving your bad relationships behind you may well be one of the biggest ones. It's also the one most people put off the longest, because to act it out in the world takes great strength of character. Picture the vision of yourself ten years from now. Is that person surrounded by jealous, resentful losers? Or does that person have a support network of other successful people to work with and guide them through life's trials and tribulations. In brief, become the kind of person you would respect and surround yourself with people of equal character.

The following does not constitute financial advice, if you require financial advice you should consult a qualified professional. Next up, budgeting. While you're young money is usually tight. It's an unfortunate truth. The good news is that if you apply the lessons from this book with what you already know, you should be more financially free later in life. Hopefully not that much later, but since you're not where you want to be yet, you'll need a plan to keep your money. Budgeting is just knowing how much you'll keep and how much you'll spend. It is the most basic and fundamental step in money management. It's not difficult, but it can be time consuming when you're starting out and aren't sure what you're doing yet. It also forces us to take a close look at our financial situation and understand exactly how wealthy, or not, we really are. For these reasons the majority of people avoid budgeting. Instead opting to spent as they please. The average UK household's unsecured debt is £15,400 according to The Guardian. Unsecured debts are things like credit cards, overdrafts, small loans, etc. It doesn't include mortgages or car loans, which are secured against the assets in question. This is the highest level of debt in history. You do not want to live beyond your means. This is especially true as a young person. For example, say you take out a £5,000 credit card with a 20% annual interest rate when you're 18 years old. You use the money and can't afford to repay it. You put it to the back of your mind and ignore the repayment letters. 10 short years later, you will owe the credit card company £36,341.27. By this point, they've probably taken action to reclaim the money owed. Likely taking you to court and charging you for the privilege, so this is a best case scenario. You'll likely have to declare bankruptcy before you've even started in life. This will make it difficult for you to move up the ladder. If you're always worried about money people can sense the desperation in you and instinctively know you're more likely to take risks and hurt others to keep yourself alive. Nobody wants to work with or give opportunities to people like that. They might not know why you're desperate, but they'll sense it. You'll understand this if you have a friend who is desperate to get into a relationship, only to scare away all of their potential partners by being too full on. They can't see what is so obvious to everyone else, and they will reject the idea if you ever suggest it to them. We all have parts of ourselves we're blind too. You can avoid a lot of the pain if you don't become desperate in any area of your life. Especially if you can avoid it. We're all attracted to strong, capable people who can be depended upon.

Budgeting helps us avoid overspending, which helps us avoid unnecessary debt, which helps us avoid financial desperation and ruin. This might sound dramatic. Just remember nobody plans to go bankrupt, the same way nobody plans to become an alcoholic, or gambling addict, etc. It happens gradually over time. You should recognise all of these things as risks in your life. You have a human nature, prone to overindulgence in the here and now. As always, because that's just part of who we are we should recognise it and have some sympathy for ourselves. It isn't necessarily a character flaw if it doesn't affect the way we live our lives. If you don't recognise the parts of yourself that could lead you down a bad path in life, you don't know yourself very well. "I'm just not the sort of person who would ever smoke/drink/over-eat/gamble/manipulate others/pretend to be wealthy" are all naive statements. I wiser person would state "I'm trying to be the type of person who can avoid the temptations of smoking/drinking/over-eating/manipulating others for personal gain/flashing my non-existent wealth by buying the latest branded clothes or phone I can't afford" etc. The wiser person understands the pleasure in the vices and what leads people to do them. The fool knows nothing of the true temptations of evil. If you have been affected by a tragedy that was partially or entirely your own fault, you understand what we're talking about here. Cheated on your partner after drinking too much? 3 stone overweight with no-one else to blame? Been fired for something you did wrong? You understand what we're talking about here. We must keep our impulses in check, and this applies to spending as much as anything else.

This is an essential part of gaining an edge on your competition. Instead of struggling with ever increasing debt, you're sitting back and watching your ever increasing wealth grow while you move towards your financial goals. Remember our credit card example? Let's reverse it. Instead of ignoring debt, you're investing money. Let's suppose you can afford to put away £1000 a month for 10 years and earn a 10% annual return on your investment. How much money do you have? £209,259.06. That might sound like a stretch right now, depending on how much you're earning. The point is that the interest compounds over time and builds your wealth. The same thing happens against you when you're in debt. Just so you know, if you could afford to put away £1000 a month for 25 years at 10% annual return, you'd have £1,349,947.29. If you did this for 50 years from age 18 to 68 (the current retirement age in the UK) you'd have £17,614,130.64. The more money you have the faster it grows, and the earlier you start the better. Once again, this isn't financial advice. It's an illustration to show you the power of saving some money regularly and not pissing it away on stuff to impress people that don't give a shit. Your friend has flashy trainers he spent 15% of his monthly paycheque on, you spent 15% of your monthly pay cheque investing and paid off your house before you were 30. Your friend is still renting at 30 (which is normal in the

UK) and moaning about how difficult it is for young people to get on the property ladder. He still has very nice trainers though. More about how all of this actually applies to you and what you can realistically do about it in the wealth section.

A crucial part of your budget should be investment in yourself. Both in terms of your time and finances. You need to dedicate a proportion of both to your personal development if you're serious about becoming the best you can be. This is another way you're going to gain an edge on your competition. Imagine if you could dedicate a small percentage of your income to investing in yourself. You use this money for books, seminars, coaching, etc. You could turn yourself into a growth machine. If you're on a low income, this will require sacrifice. However, this is an investment. It's not usual expenditure. The money you invest here should come back to you many, many times over. We recommend opening a separate savings account for free with your existing bank and labelling it your personal development fund. You can easily set up a standing order to sweep a percentage of each month's pay cheque into the account or just do this manually if you're paid irregularly. Commit to spending an amount of all the money you bring in on making yourself a more developed and complete person. Having the money sitting there waiting makes it easier to spend it on the right things. Say you're going for a big promotion at work and could use some 1:1 support and coaching from a professional to help you land the job. That might cost you £500.

This seems like a lot, until you factor in that the promotion earns you another £6000 a year. You've recovered your £500 investment in one month and banked £5500 profit that year. That's a good return on investment in anyone's eyes. Say you're looking to learn from the best and attend seminars lead by people who have mastered exactly what you're looking to do. Perhaps the seminar ticket, travel and hotel stay costs you £500. The same logic applies. Perhaps you've seen the value in audio books. Your favourite audiobook company offers a discount if you pay for an annual subscription upfront. It seems like a lot of money, but the knowledge contained in the books will allow you to become the best person you can be with far higher earning potential. Hopefully you can see the importance of this step. They say you have to spend money to make money, so spend it wisely.

Get up. Dress Up. Show up. It doesn't matter how you feel. There will be days where you don't want to put in the effort. That's fine. But you show up and look the part. This is as simple as it gets. People notice that you're consistently well dressed and turn up every single day. This doesn't mean you should overexert yourself and work ungodly hours for years to try and impress your superiors while earning a pitiful wage. This book isn't about any of that. However, your reputation can make or break you. People notice when you make the effort, even if they never tell you. You should aim to be the best dressed person in the room. Do not be too flashy. Best dressed does not mean you're dripping in branded tackiness. That makes you look cheap and unsophisticated. It means your clothes fit you and are appropriate for your industry. You're clean and presentable. You're not showing off, you're making a reasonable effort to let everyone know you take yourself and your job seriously. One last time: don't show off. Spend a few hours watching some style videos on Youtube. A personal favourite of mine is Alpha M for men's style, fashion and grooming tips. He helped me a lot as a younger man. Ladies resources are numerous and endless. Nail down the basics first. Kept hair, cut your nails, be clean, smell nice. Wear clothes that fit you, nothing too baggy or excessively tight. Keep your shoes clean. You do not have to spend a fortune to look nice. Use what you have and don't be afraid to buy 2nd hand if money is tight. There are many discount clothing stores in the UK these days too. Remember, the point is to present yourself nicely. Nobody knows or cares how much your clothes cost, unless you put this on display because you think it will impress people. Top tip here, most people in your workplace and social circles have a good idea of roughly how much you earn. If you're carrying the latest iPhone and a £2000 bag, but you earn £20,000 a year, people just think you're a dick. They think you're trying to be better than them, and assume you're bad with money or that your daddy or partner paid for your stuff. Nobody thinks you're balling. You're allowed nice things, you just shouldn't be using them to try and assert some kind of financial dominance over your co-workers, especially when everyone knows you can't afford it. Not cool. Finally on this topic, do not overexpose yourself physically, it doesn't matter how long you've spent in the gym. Unless you're a personal trainer you should not be wearing spray on trousers or exposing too much skin. Even if you are a personal trainer, exercise caution here. Why? You're being unprofessional. Professionals are courteous to people they work with, they're conscientious and generally business like. This might be who you are, and power to you. However, this is a book for young professionals. People who want to become highly paid professionals. No surprises for knowing that you don't become a highly paid professional by being unprofessional. Deal with it, or find another way to make your money where you don't have to be courteous to people or conscientious of your actions and how you affect others. Perhaps you'd rather be an Instagram model?

Don't have kids yet. Children are incredibly rewarding independent beings. They will bring you endless joy, heartache, love, worry and real undeniable meaning in life. They are infinitely worthwhile and without them, you will feel the lack in later life. With all that said: Do. Not. Rush. You're trying to achieve great things in life, and despite what all the magazines and talk shows tell you (especially if you're a young woman), it's really hard to do it all. You're going to need to work full time to apply the lessons of this book and reach higher career success, at least in the beginning. Lots of people are comfortable farming out the raising of their children to nannies and others. If your child is in care or school for 50+ hours each week, and you're only seeing them for an hour or two each day, why are you having them? Seriously, get a dog. In fact, I don't even recommend you treat the dog like that. 50+ hours a week in kennels and special time occasionally in the evenings (when you're not exhausted and snappy, which will be a lot) and resentful weekends… I don't believe anyone wants to do this on purpose, but it's worth properly planning out because we're talking about someone else's life here. A precious little life that shouldn't be an afterthought. Too many children are left unattended to in important ways so their parents can pursue narrow minded success. Your vision of success should change when you have children by the way, because it shouldn't be all about you anymore. This sounds obvious, but millions of children are suffering right now because their parents thing they can "have it all". The high paying job, the nice house, the children, the flash car, the luxury holidays every few months. News flash: the life you want takes time to build. You can't have it all until you've earned it and worked hard for it. You can't have it just because you want it. If you do too much too soon, everything will suffer. Including and especially your children. There's just no way to sugar coat this. You need to build up to this gradually over time. If you can't keep your laundry clean and hold down a 20k job without feeling exhausted 24/7, what on earth makes you think you're ready to add some children into the mix? Just hold on a while, all things in good time. Please don't be the parents who are both working from 8am to 6pm who rarely spend any time with their children, yet alone give them any genuine careful attention necessary for their development. Then have the audacity to wonder why their little cherubs reach adolescence and become overanxious, or unambitious, or lazy, or unproductively rebellious or druggies. These parents say, "We gave them everything, the nice home, safe neighbourhood, great schooling, extra curriculars, clubs" and "we just don't understand, we've tried everything (we've paid for everything we can think of)". These children are at severe risk of being labelled with some kind of mental illness, ADHD and other learning difficulties are very popular these days. These parents are often desperate to blame their unloved child's shortcomings on this illness. Doomed child is then saddled with blame and limiting belief for the rest of their days - unless they realise what their well-meaning foolish parents have done. The narrative of "you can have it all", particularly aimed at young women, has done irreconcilable damage. Plan out exactly how much time you'll be able to spend with your child in the first 5 years of their life. This is assuming you stay with your partner, and they don't regularly work away. According to the office of national statistics, 53% of couples who marry before the age of 20 will separate, compared with 23% who marry between 30-34, and 7% who marry between 45-49. Nobody who gets married plans to get divorced by the way (gold diggers aside). I'm stating these figures because everyone reading this book is mature enough to recognise that they're not the exception to the rule. This is just divorce figures by the way, figures for separation and break ups outside of marriage are much higher. Unfortunately, all this considered, you're more likely to separate from your partner than stay with them if you're a younger person these days. The point of highlighting this is to make it clear that if you're having children before 30, statistically the person you had those children with won't be around when they turn 16. Just keep it in mind. Also according to the ONS, over two thirds of divorces are petitioned by women. Let's run through a typical example. You'll be working from 8am to 6pm, your partner will be doing something similar or isn't around. Your child will be awake from around 6am to 6pm in the first 2 years of life, and perhaps until 7pm in the 3rd to 5th years of their life. You have no plans to cut down or change your working hours and neither does your partner. Your children will be visiting you or your ex-partner the weekends depending on what you agreed in the settlement. If you get to see your kids at the weekends you're typically paying the child support to the other person. Probably 25% of your income. If you don't get to see your children at the weekend, when are you spending any time with them? During the week you realise you must rely on family help, au pairs, child minders etc to raise *your* child. Ask yourself if this is fair for the child. Ask yourself again. Ask yourself one more time. The idea of spending any time at home with your own children is seen as disgustingly outdated and oppressive in today's media, especially if you're a woman. Don't be fooled here. Think long and hard before having children, especially if you're going to do so before you're 30. The odds are seriously against you and against your child. If you need any further motivation, you can google the statistics for child development for single parent households in comparison to co-parenting households. It is 2020 and you're trying to become a mature adult. Treat this decision accordingly.

Don't buy a house to live in. This shouldn't be confused with, "don't buy a house". Property can be a great investment at the right time in your life. However, for the reasons we'll soon discuss around location mobility you do not want to be tied down anywhere while you're young. Any property you invest in should be just that, an investment. There are plenty of living hacks you can use to minimise housing expenses and maximise your return on investment. I bought my first property at 20. I spent the next few months renovating it while living in it and went on to get three bedrooms from the two bedroom property. I rented out two of those rooms to fully cover my mortgage costs and my living expenses. I then got a job which required me to move away, and I had the freedom to do it easily knowing I didn't have to find the money for expensive mortgage payments or worry about selling the property. If I'd have bought the property as a home for myself, it could have prevented me from taking a great promotion on a lot more money. I'd designed this investment to work for me in line with my 10 year vision. They'll come a time when you can afford to finance and build your own dream home if that's what you want, but right now your location mobility and ability to respond to opportunities quickly is more valuable to you than a home that anchors you to a single location. True that it's possible to sell your home when you need to, but have you ever sold a home? It's almost always a 3-month process minimum. That job that doubles your salary might not still be there in 3 months. Once you're senior enough they'll be paying your relocation expenses handsomely, but you're getting nowhere slowly if you're waiting for that opportunity fresh out of school. Much better to rent as a young person, it gives you the freedom you need. Consider renting a room in a house yourself if you want to keep costs low. You can use the money you save to invest and get on the property ladder. As a general rule you don't want to anchor yourself anywhere until you've lived a multitude of places and know where you want to settle and start your family. By the time you reach that point, you should be demanding a wage that suits you and have employers competing for you so you can work wherever you like. Until you reach that point, you're probably settling for less than you deserve and limiting your options to do it. You have your reasons, spouses, desire for children and a million other pressures. Just know that you're giving up one of your greatest assets as a young person once you settle down and limit yourself to one area.

Don't hate the successful. This sounds obvious, because you're going to become a successful person. However, watch how you act towards the successful. Have you ever seen someone in a really nice car and made a comment to your friends about how that person must be compensating for something? Do you think politicians, company directors and the people who run things are all out of touch and corrupt, perhaps you've even told your friends those people are wankers or something similar. Have you ever complained about how much footballers are paid? Do you see a piece of art that's sold for several million pounds and assume the artist is having a joke at everyone else's expense, or have you ever said "anyone could have done that (piece of art)". If you answered yes to any of the above, there's a strong chance you have some hate for the successful. Your immediate reaction will likely be to dismiss the fact, but this is a limiting belief and will hold you back, whether you're conscious of it or not. You'll need to face this. The good news is that like all beliefs, it can be changed. We need to look up to successful people and respect that they've been able to do something we haven't. You don't have to like everyone, or everything they do. However, have some respect for what they've been able to achieve and don't bring them down to make yourself feel better. Which is exactly what's happening when we make comments like the above. The obvious exception here is if the successful person is clearly immoral and actually corrupt. However even in that case, the act of hating them and not taking any action against them directly is a waste of your resources. You moaning about a politician or director of your company just makes you look resentful and jealous, even if you think people openly agree with you. Nobody wants to promote moany mc-my-problems-are-everyone-else's-fault. Even if you never openly voice your hatred, the fact it's taking up space in your head and is a negative belief will hold you down. It's a poor person's mindset. If you keep a poor person's mindset, you'll keep being poor. As eluded to earlier, you're going to be one of these powerful high earners one day, or you'll be working very closely with them to earn the money you want. Power isn't any easy thing to hold. To keep hold of it you need to keep a lot of people happy. This causes powerful people to make decisions that average people can't understand. They do it to keep the people who keep them in power happy. You would have to do the same thing in their shoes, or the people who keep you in power would remove you. Internalise this point. Consider it until it makes sense. There's a simple but insightful video by CGP Grey on Youtube: Rules for Rulers. If you're interested in power, and why the people who have it behave as they do, watch it. It's a great introduction to a complicated and extensive topic. The important point here is that people who earn more money and have more power than you have to face problems you can't even conceive of from where you're standing. Don't judge them from your position too quickly. Put yourself in their shoes, imagine having the pressures they have. It's important to remember they're just people, with the same imperfect nature as the rest of us. This doesn't mean that it's alright to lie or make immoral decisions.

Perhaps it's not a moral argument that makes you hate the successful, but instead jealousy. This is more likely if you're older and unsuccessful, and hopefully it doesn't apply to most readers here. However if this is the case, you must consult yourself and dispense with these emotions. There is no reason to be jealous. You can have everything they have. You know it. You just need to work for it over time. If you're not sure whether you're jealous, ask yourself if you talk shit behind people's backs. Particularly if it's about them being better than you in some way. "Jackie's always cutting corners and pretending to do more work than everyone else" is a negative way of admitting that she just does more work than you. "Ashraf's always kissing up to the boss" is a good way of telling everyone that you see Ashraf has a good relationship with his boss and that you don't like it. The examples are universal and a bit cliched, but they prove a point. Do you gossip about people? This probably means you're jealous. It needs to stop. You'll find middle aged unsuccessful people gossip a lot. This is why: they're sick to the teeth of seeing their unrealised potential in everyone else. You're likely the sort of person who isn't consumed with jealousy and resentment, and it's important to stay that way. One of the best ways to avoid this is to make sure you're living up to your potential and staying on the right path. If you don't, you'll lay yourself open to the temptations of bringing other people down to make yourself feel better. You might not have the spine to bully them to their face, and will likely gossip behind their back out of jealousy. Avoid this.

Conversely, if you find people are talking about you behind your back or you otherwise have some "haters" this might actually be a good thing. It could mean that you've got a serious attitude problem and need to grow up. Likely though, if you're living a life true to who you are and following the steps in this book, you have a different problem. You're rubbing people up the wrong way because they see your potential, your intelligence, your youth, and they cannot stand to compare themselves to you. These are the people who will take any opportunity to jab at your character and try to make you second guess everything you do. If you're a great person, you'll encounter this all the time. The critics can seem louder than your supporters at times. Learn to recognise the difference between people who want the best for you, and people who just want to bring you down. You have a responsibility to yourself to stay true to who you are at all costs. Let the jealous losers hate all they want; they can't hurt you. Never become one of those people. They're where they are for a reason. Their own inaction, insecurities and lack of willingness to adopt responsibility. You should be kind and supportive to these people in all situations, but more on dealing with difficult relationships soon.

Location mobility. This will give you an advantage over people unwilling to move for work. Keep in mind though, this won't be necessary in all professions. Increasingly companies are utilising technology to reduce the travel expenditure of their employees. You can connect remotely to all your meetings if your organisation is progressive enough. For those of you who already work this way, you know there are strong arguments against this style; mainly that face-to-face contact bonds people and leads to more collaborative teams. For the purposes of this chapter we're not interested in the science of it right now. The point is that it is more than possible to work somewhere you only visit once a month or less. Generally speaking, the more senior you become the more control you will have over your own schedule and location. If this is something that's really important to you, you've probably already factored it into your career choice. This sounds great but the truth is that once you're experienced enough there will be a demand for your services wherever you want to go. After all the world over needs skilled doctors, engineers and project managers alike.

Technology is great at reducing travel requirements and enabling virtual location freedom. However, in the early days of your career you'll need to be where the opportunities are. This doesn't mean you immediately up sticks and plant yourself in the largest metropolitan hub you can find. It means you're willing to follow the opportunities when they come your way and move for the right position. In short, you're going to have to move. You likely already understand and appreciate this if you've attended a university outside your hometown. You need to move to get what you want sometimes. The thing is, when you're young you don't have much bargaining power with the people paying you. You're relatively inexperienced and they're taking a bit of a gamble employing you. Even if you're the next prodigy of your industry, respect the fact you need to prove yourself and earn your wings. For these reasons it's difficult to get a leg up the ladder sometimes. You need to play to your strengths. One thing you do have over the more established older generations is a less established life. When people reach middle age, they have generally established caring responsibilities for children or spouses or elderly parents. They've anchored themselves to one location with a large house and equally large mortgage payments. They have a network of friends they're trying to impress. If they're earning good money, chances are themselves and their spouse have become accustomed to a certain type of lifestyle, perhaps two expensive cars with large finance payments and a couple of holidays a year, meals out are a regular thing, the kids are in a lovely (but quite expensive) school. All of this is great by the way, people work hard for their money and we should respect their choice to spent it how they please. The point is that when you're young, you're usually only responsible for yourself. You need to take full advantage of this while you still can. Children and partners and pets are wonderful, rewarding responsibilities that will make you put their interests ahead of your own. This means you're at a disadvantage to the people who have nobody to think about but themselves. Make the most of not having all of these things in your life, so that you can fully appreciate and embrace them when you do have them in your life. Set yourself up well early. Be willing to move at the start of your career. You have less to loose right now than at any other time in your life. Once you have the skills and experience you can leverage them so that the high paying work comes to you.

Chapter 6

Interviews & Applications

You're ready. It's time to start bringing home some more money. You're packing some serious knowledge; you're armed and ready. It's time to apply our skills to the art of a successful interview. Unless you're just starting out or right at the top of the pyramid, you're likely going to have to interview for positions. Sometimes you can line up a job where the interview is a formality. Most of the time in today's world of employer accountability and the threat of tribunals, the application and interview process is a mostly fair and meritocratic process – the best person wins. So, you'll need to know how to develop the best application and give the best interview(s) possible. Luckily this is a skill like any other, and it can be learnt.

Some people consider themselves naturally introverted and find it difficult to sell themselves in an interview. Considering it disingenuous to oversell themselves, lacking the confidence to really highlight their strengths.

This is very common. It's ok. Part of the reason for the first few chapters was to lead you to the point where you're willing to demand better for yourself, as if you really deserve it as much as anyone else. Key message: take yourself seriously and treat yourself with some respect. If you properly embrace this way of life and have assessed your strengths and weaknesses, you should have no trouble honestly telling someone about yourself in an interview. You now know who you are and what you're doing. You don't need to fool anyone because you understand exactly who you are and your true value. If you've skipped ahead to this point in the book without reading the first chapters and following the exercises, I have some bad news. There are no secret magic beans here. The key is developing yourself in the ways we've already discussed. The courage to look someone dead in the eye and speak honestly is a superpower. In the long term it will get you further than trickery, allow you to live your best life true to who you really are, and be a force for good in the world around you.

I will share all the techniques and a comprehensive framework for landing your next job here. Just do not try to skip past the steps mentioned so far. If you do, the techniques will work and you will build a shallow life of success destined for collapse. You'll climb a ladder that's propped up against the wrong wall in foundations of sand. Your power crazed manager on their second divorce did that. Your scandalous government officials, corrupt police officers and negligent parents all did that.

Don't be like these people. Live a life with meaning and purpose for the reasons we've already discussed. It pays off, I promise.

Alright next on the agenda is finding a promotion. This just means a job that pays more than your current one. It doesn't mean directly moving up one place in the chain of command in your current workplace. It can mean this too, but you'll be waiting a LONG time if this is your direct career development strategy. You should take these excellent opportunities when they present themselves. However, if you only want your bosses' job, or a more senior version of your own, you'll have to wait a long time to progress. Particularly if the position you want is filled by someone competent in the eyes of their superiors, and the persons in those positions have no desire to move on. So, keep your horizons broad and your options open.

Moving around different companies, or different areas of your own if it's sufficiently large, is the fastest way to earn more money. It's the fastest way to build reputation and a credible CV too. Multiple high responsibility positions in the same company is the holy grail, it shows you're competent and trustworthy and highly valued by your company. The thing is that if you work for a large corporate, the different departments are often so separate from each other they're like different companies. I have personally worked for one of the UK's largest banks. Within this company even the business departments rarely spoke to each other. Let alone the retail bank, car finance or pensions departments. You can use this to your advantage. Not getting a promotion in your current department quick enough? You can just move. Move departments to another role that fits your 10-year vision that pays more.

This sounds simple, but for the location mobility and other reasons already discussed, young people all too often anchor themselves to one place. There's also the issue that if you're good, your company will groom you to stay in your current position as long as possible. Offering promotions and pay increases on the horizon, but always just around the corner. Here's a lesson I wish I'd learned sooner. Business is business. It's never personal. For example, say you work in customer service for an energy company. If you're an excellent telephone handler with relevant knowledge, your superiors will often tell you you're not ready to move on because they can't afford to lose you. With very few exceptions, someone will always be willing to pay you more than you're earning right now. If you can fill a void for someone, they'll pay you for it. This doesn't mean it's the right thing to do to jump ship every time someone's offering a few thousand more a year. However, do not get caught in the mentality that you're stuck in your current workplace or position. If someone gave you your job at your current company, someone will give you a job elsewhere.

If you have no experience or are reading this before landing your first fulltime job, don't worry. You're actually at a great advantage. You have the power to negotiate the highest starting salary possible. This is important because the salary you start on will usually dictate your earning power for years to come. As a basic example, it's far easier to land a £40,000 a year job if you're already earning £30,000. You have further to go if you're currently earning £18,000. This shouldn't hold people back, but it does. You have to start somewhere, so apply the lessons here to start as far up the ladder as possible.

When looking for a promotion, it's bad practice to look for one perfect job. You want to line up at least 5 different interviews, which probably means applying for at least 10 jobs if your CV is incredible and cover letter on point. You can cut down on your number of applications significantly if you already know someone in the area you want to work. More about this in the networking section. For now, let's assume you're submitting cold applications (you don't know someone already working there). This is a perfectly acceptable strategy for positions that aren't too senior, or where more than one of that type of position exists. You'll land a job in the military, as a pilot, or doctor, or salesperson, so on, without personal recommendation. This is generally true for technical positions where they're employing you for a specific skill you have, or entry to middle level positions. You generally won't land a job as a senior manager, or anything heavily people based or senior, without strong personal recommendations from people already in the company. We'll address how to build a network to benefit your career in that section of the book. Just know that once you have one it will help significantly, and there's no way around it if you want to be a success.

For now though, back to interviews and applications. You already know your career path and the next 12 months of your life. You need to shortlist 10 different positions which will get you on the path to where you need to be. Use jobs websites and social media. Check out the websites of any companies you particularly like for their open positions. Contact them directly if they don't have a section on their website to ask if they're hiring. Ask your existing network of friends and family if they know of any positions, and your professional network if you've established one. Work with what you can find. Don't panic too much about position and salary right now, you can work upwards from here and negotiate salary before taking a job in any case. This is the first step of many upwards in your career. Shortlist 10 jobs you like the look of that fit with your 10 year vision.

CV. Your "Curriculum Vitae" or "Rèsumè" is the best advertisement you have of your skills and experience. There's a lot of advice available online about these, but free advice is usually worth exactly what you pay for it. In truth everyone has a different take on the CV, and this is a good thing. It's supposed to be a representation of your unique background, skills and experience after all. That said some universal advice applies here. This both from my perspective as a hiring manager for large companies at multiple levels, the tried and tested experience of my peers, and the available literature on the subject.

1. Keep it brief. Nobody has time to read your life story and a complete overview of your roles and responsibilities of every job you've had since high school. It's dull. I've probably got 50 applications on my desk. If I can't see what makes you suitable for the job in 30 seconds, I'm moving on to someone who's more articulate and a better communicator. If it's relevant to the job you're applying for include it in your personal statement section, skills section, or your cover letter. As a rule, 2 pages is a lot. 1 page is best. Including an appendix for your qualifications is acceptable and this shouldn't be included in your page count.

2. Career history. It should be obvious from your job title what your position entailed. Nobody knows or has time to ponder what the chief business officer of central group program liaisons at District Factors Ltd does, and nobody cares either. You can and should change your old job titles to something recognisable on your CV. You can jazz them up too, as long as they're still accurately and fairly representing what you actually did. If you were a call handler at a phone company for a long time –

Senior Telephony Customer Relationship Manager at Fancy Mobile Phones Ltd is more than acceptable. Do. Not. Lie. Just make it obvious what you were doing and ensure the job title is a genuine and fair summary of that. Without stating the obvious, don't ever change the name of the company you worked for.

3. You need a personal summary, and it needs to be at the top of your CV. It should be short and sweet. 150 – 300 words. Sum up why you're the best thing since sliced bread with your unique skills and experience. Don't use filler words and work to get some personality into it. "I am passionate about customer service" is generic. "I learned to make friends quickly in school and this is still one of my biggest strengths today. I'm good at getting to know people and asking the right questions to get people to really open up." is immeasurably better. Build your personality into your personal statement and keep it brief.

4. Ask for help from people who hire other people. Everyone has their opinion, your parents and friends, but only consult people who know what they're talking about. Pay for their advice if you have to. Don't ask people who don't have relevant experience of reviewing CVs, even if they're well meaning. You'll get too much advice and won't be able to sort the functional from the misleading at

this stage in your career. If you have a mentor (more on that later) then ask them.

Cover letters. Most large companies are moving their application processes online these days, so you might not be expected to write a cover letter per se. However, there will be a box labelled "Tell us why you think your skills and experience make you a suitable candidate for this position" or something similar. This section is where you put your cover letter. The quality of people's cover letters on average is so poor, some companies will ask you to fill out multiple boxes on their application website with questions like "What do you see as the value of customer service?" and "Discuss the importance of team work"... which is sad but just something we're going to have to work with. Essentially, you'll need two things to write a good cover letter. A good understanding of your overall skills, strengths and weaknesses, and a copy of the job description. You're going to fail if you don't have either of these. Here's a top tip, if the job description is too vague and brief, they likely don't want you to apply for the job and already have someone else lined up for it. OR the hiring manager is inept and a terrible communicator, and therefore almost certainly someone you don't want to work with. OR the company has a terrible generic template for job applications. All of these are red flags. Stay away. Genuine good companies work hard to attract talented people. The job description should be appropriately detailed for the level of salary it offers. It won't necessarily be very readable and will probably contain company jargon you couldn't possibly understand (unless you've worked at that company for 5 years). That's more acceptable and something you can at least work with. The point is this, you absolutely must have a firm grasp on what the job entails before you apply for it. Otherwise you're wasting your time trying to guess what someone else wants from you.

You need to write a bespoke cover letter for each role you apply for. Now if you apply for multiple similar roles you'll be able to use a lot of the same material, but you should still ensure it's bespoke. Mention the specific job role and the company you're applying for several times as you write your cover letter. A great general format is to start with a personal summary of who you are, your skills and experience. This should be different to the personal summary on your CV. Hiring managers don't want to hire someone lazy. Make the effort to rephrase your personal summary in a more specific format for the role in question. After this, bring out your analysis of your strengths and weaknesses from earlier, and keep a printed copy of the job description next to it. Work through the job description and try to include a breakdown of why your strengths and experience cover all points included in the job spec. Be honest about the knowledge you don't have. If you go for an engineering position and it requires knowledge of a specific sort of software you haven't used, don't lie about that. Explain that you've used multiple different software programmes and are very computer literate, but that you haven't got experience with that particular programme. You're willing to learn, perhaps you mention you've looked into the software online and seen some tutorials and you're comfortable you'll pick it up fast. This is far more impressive than lying. After you've nailed all the key elements of the job spec, you'll need to write a conclusion. Use this to sum up your key strengths you want to reemphasise. Repeating key points using slightly different language will help reinforce your point. What you're trying to get across is more likely to stick in the hiring manager's head if you say it more than once. Keep it succinct. Remember, you're trying to get across that you're a good communicator. Nobody likes sifting through endless waffle, get to the point. Always finish by giving the hiring manager the impression that you expect to be seriously considered for the position, without explicitly saying it. "Thank you for taking the time to review my application. I look forward to hearing from you and would be happy to answer any further question you may have." is sufficient to make the right impression. End the letter with "Sincerely [insert your name]" if you addressed the letter to an individual hiring manager. End the letter with "Faithfully [insert your name]" if you do not know the name of the hiring manager.

This is an art, not a science. A good job application is something that takes time and experience to hone. You now have the skills and knowledge to write something compelling. Practice. Don't use the same CV or cover letter wording for every job. It can be immensely useful to put out 20 or 30 applications using a separate style for every 5 or so applications. Then note which style gets you the most interview offers. Use this as your basis going forward. This isn't necessary but if you're just starting out and haven't had more than 5 interviews in your life, it will likely help you refine your skills and pay dividends for the rest of your career. Get credible people you trust to review your applications. Mentors or other professionals. Credible organisations. Etc. Your direct line of management probably isn't the best resource of support - unless they're directly offering to support you in getting a promotion. The reason for this is simple. If they think you're going to abandon them, they'll stop investing in you. Who wants to recognise and reward a deserter? It's a sad truth. You'll notice your performance reviews becoming more critical. Your 1:1's with your manager pushed back and rescheduled more regularly. Occasionally you'll find a good manager who wants the best for you, but all too often (particularly at lower levels of management) they're only trying to look after their own interest and impress their superiors. The minute you hint that you're leaving, you're disposable. The best thing to do is source your promotion independently. Once you have a job offer, you can always bring this back to the negotiating table to leverage a high salary or better hours etc.

In fact, that's a wise thing to do. For now though, consult your current line manager as little as possible unless you have complete trust that they have your best interests at heart (no matter the costs to them).

Interview questions and preparation. Congrats, your excellent job application skills have landed you some interviews. This is the make or break of the process. You can take your time polishing a job application. In the interview you won't have the luxury of unbounded thinking time. It's the difference between leisurely texting someone and being on a first date. Time to back up everything you said on your application with solid delivery, charisma and charm. It's usually not possible to know exactly which questions will be asked of you prior to your interview. Luckily though, there's a fairly fool proof method of preparing great answers that will cover you in almost all eventualities. You'll need to put in some preparation time. The higher paying the job, the better you'll need to prepare. However, it's more than possible to have all the answers you'll need in your back pocket for an interview. This is what successful people do. You don't need to be the quickest thinking of memory recall champions. You just need to be a normal person who knows what they're going to say ahead of time.

A lot of the nerves in an interview setting come from the uncertainty of it all. We just don't know if we're going to be able to impress these people. The power seems totally on the other side of the desk and it can be intimidating.

We tell ourselves we just don't know what they're looking for. We don't know how to answer their question. Believe it or not, interviews can be enjoyable and engaging experiences. Particularly if the hiring manager wants you to do well, which they should, because they're going to be working with you (or another person in your exact situation) very closely soon. Proper preparation we're about to discuss will allow you the luxury of comfort in the interview seat. You'll have a quiet confidence because you'll know what they're looking for. You'll know how to answer any questions that come up. You're offering the person interviewing you something powerful, your individual skills and experience. You're offering them your man power, your intelligence, a significant proportion of your time. You recognise these things are truly valuable and that the power sits with you. If this particular interviewer doesn't recognise your skills, that's fine. You'll have sharpened your communication skills in the process and will go on to better offer your services to someone else who will recognise your talent. You're not arrogant, you're quietly self-assured by being confident in your own abilities.

There are some fundamentals to interviews:

1. Find out as much about the company as possible. You may well be outright asked what you know about the company. You should understand what they do. For everything except school leaver posi-

tions, this is non-negotiable. Recruitment agencies may try to keep this information from you. Explain you're not interested in the position unless they give you a full brief on the company and tell you who you'll be working for. It's that important. There are a couple of reasons for this. You'll likely be asked outright what you know about the company. If you're not asked outright, you can make your interview stand out by preparing your answers carefully. Splice specific information about the company into your answers. Research this information by looking at the company's website, social media pages, google map their location(s). Are they a large company? Do they service the end consumer directly or do they deal exclusively with other businesses? Do they make a product? Do they provide a service? What can you find out about said products or services? Don't overlook basic information like this. I had an interview with a well known luxury car company early in my career. The interviewer asked me what I knew about the company. I told him that I liked the company a lot and didn't know all that much about how it worked. He sniffed, looked down his nose into my eyes and exclaimed "We're a luxury German car company". I was dismissed from that moment on as uneducated and incompetent. He listened with all the attention and expression one gives someone else's crying child in a restaurant for the rest of the interview. Now, I've always been very interested in cars, and I certainly knew that company was German and made expensive cars. I made the mistake of assuming the interviewer wasn't looking for an obvious answer. Don't overlook the obvious here. If you're applying for an engineering company, state that you know it's an engineering company. All the better if you can find information on the company's values, customer service philosophy, their mission statement, where in the world they do business etc. Don't overlook the basics or assume anything.

2. You need to speak to the interviewer with full respect, but as if you're explaining all your answers to an Alien who has no concept of planet earth. Really. You need to explain everything. Assume nothing. Your non-verbal communication is important, but it will not save you if your verbal communication is off topic. The reason is because the interviewer is likely making notes as if their life depends on it. In a way, their job depends on it. In today's world of employment tribunals and lawsuits, everything has to be evidenced. When they offer you the job based on your answers, they'll need to evidence why your interview was better than the others. You must give them tangible verbal answers which can be written down. Anything you imply will not be written down, no matter how

strongly. If you don't say it explicitly, you basically never said it. Secondly, they (usually) don't know you. They have different experiences, different lives. They don't understand you, although if they're good they'll try to make you feel like they do. They don't know that you've been working an extra hour at work every day for the last 3 years. They don't know about the relationship you have with your manager. They don't know how well respected you are amongst your peers. They don't know your company lingo. It's your job to get everything across. When you explain things, do it clearly and completely. With full respect, take that person with you on a journey through all your experiences.

3. The STAR methodology. This is industry standard format for answering questions. It takes practice. If you don't use it, or something similar, you'll fail. It works on the principal that when you're asked a question, you give a specific example of a time when you faced the problem posed in the question. You then walk the interviewer through that example, to evidence that you understand how to deal with that specific thing. An example question might be: "How would you deal with a particularly difficult customer?". You do not answer the question directly. Instead, you speak about a specific time you did deal with a particularly difficult cus-

tomer. This is better, it proves you've got experience and know what you're doing. If you haven't worked with customers, you'd outline how you dealt with a difficult person. Or when you were a customer and received excellent service. The point is that you talk about real experiences that you've had. No fluffy philosophy. Using the following format:

Situation:

Outline where you were and what was happening. Give the whole thing some context.

Task:

This is what you were supposed to be doing at the time. What were you doing when this happened?

Action:

What action did you specifically take when this situation came up. Avoid "we" or "my team and I". Tell the interviewer what *you* did exactly.

Result:

As a result of the action you took, what exactly happened? Always make sure the result was good or better than the standard outcome. You can actually give negative results if you learned a valuable lesson doing the thing but be measured here. This will be important for more senior interviews. BUT Always include another example of how you applied the learning from your mistakes. Never end on a true negative.

Let's work through an example.

Interview question: How would you deal with a particularly difficult customer?

Your answer:

S: I was working in a high street branch of a big mobile phone company. I had an elderly customer try to return a phone on a contract that was outside the cooling off period. We allow customers 14 days to cancel their contracts but after this point they're locked in. It was obvious to me the customer had been oversold this product, it was the latest iPhone but the customer had difficulty seeing and hearing. He was visibly quite upset and at times became angry and somewhat confused.

T: It was policy to send them away and give them the details of our complaints department.

A: I knew complaints wouldn't help because the product was outside the cooling off window. It was unlikely they would understand over the phone that the product may have been miss-sold. The customer was a proud man and wouldn't admit he couldn't use this type of phone properly with his eyesight and possible dementia. I felt compassion for the customer. I spoke to my manager. Initially they didn't want to accept the cancellation/return as it was against policy. I used my influencing skills to appeal to my manager's better nature, and we agreed to change the customer's contract to something much more suitable and affordable, and swap the handset to something more basic with large buttons. I carefully discussed this with the customer.

R: The customer was overjoyed with the solution we proposed. The branch didn't have to record any negative sales figures from the return and everyone left the situation happy. I showed the customer how to operate their new handset and moved all their numbers and information across. He thanked me for my time. My manager at the time was impressed with the solution and I went on to receive written recognition which went towards me being nominated for an award later in the year.

You can clearly see how this answer says more than any amount of waffle about how you feel customer service is important. It's a tangible example of what you've done and results you've had with real people. Explain the situation, the task you were meant to be doing, the actions you actually took, and the direct results of your actions. That's the STAR technique. Use this to answer all the questions asked of you. Use a real world example.

How to know what you'll be asked. If you're going for a job inside your company, there will often be a standard interview format you can use. Check the managers section of your company intranet/internal websites. Otherwise ask a senior person who isn't in your direct line of management. The interview format may change depending on the grade of job you're applying for. This is the easiest way. Often things won't be this straightforward. Instead you'll need to employ some thought power. Firstly, put yourself in the employer's shoes. Before we start expending too much brain power trying to consider what they might ask us (we'll get to that); ask where they're going to get their interview questions from. Hiring managers don't sit around drafting their own interview questions for every position they advertise. As a rule, they'll have a large script of potential questions to ask. They just pick the most appropriate ones to ask. Oftentimes in large companies it's mandated that they ask you certain questions to ensure a fair interview experience for all candidates. All the better, this makes your life easier. Large companies have probably had an in-house specialist draft up the questions at some point. Run a google search for "Interview template [insert company name]". You'll be shocked at how often companies publish their own interview questions. If not, someone has almost undoubtably published the potential questions independently. Websites like Glassdoor, Reddit, and other user contribution forums can be gold. If the company isn't very large, they might not have a standard interview format for you to go through. In this case, there's a high probability the directors have done an online search for: "Best interview questions for small companies" or "Best interview questions for [insert industry name and/or job title]". The people running these companies aren't all super geniuses, they're just people. Smart people who want to make their lives as easy as possible.

Alright so we've cut a corner by not expending needless energy thinking up every possible question. Next up, find the job spec for the role. Have a look through it. You're likely to be asked questions based around this document. This is, after all, a description of your role and future responsibilities. Go through and make sure you're comfortable covering all bases. Look through the role specific experience/qualities you'll need. Ensure you've got a STAR answer in the bag for these. If you don't have a qualification it says would be desirable, better think of a STAR response for why you have the relevant knowhow or experience. If you need specific knowledge of a system, or industry, etc, better think of a STAR response that fits. STAR responses are like learning any new skill. Like learning to play a song on the guitar for instance. It's going to be difficult the first time you do it, you'll be all over the place and a bit forced and rusty. The more you practice, the easier it will get, and the better you'll become. It won't be painful for long, but you'll probably suck in the beginning. This is absolutely ok. It's actually essential to your success. Most people find it difficult, so they give up before they've given themselves a chance to get good. This is where you stand out from the crowd. You train yourself to become a competent speaker and master the art of taking someone through your past experiences with you on a personal level. You become a storyteller.

You don't just get good at answering interview questions, you get good at communicating with people. This skill above almost all others will contribute to your success in the largest way.

Challenge time. For the next 3 weeks, set aside 20 minutes a day. This is work related, so squeeze this into your working day as personal development (easier in a desk job with nobody looking over your shoulder), or take the time out of your lunch break. Commit to doing this for 21 days straight. You're going to write a STAR interview answer. To make this even easier, I've included 21 of the most common interview questions you'll be asked. The point isn't the questions. The point is to increase your fluency in communicating in this style. When you come to an interview you'll find it x10 easier to prepare if you've done this exercise. You'll have mastered a skill most give up on day 1. Keep in mind that nailing the right interview can increase your income by tens of thousands. You should treat it accordingly and prepare as such. There's no right or wrong answers here, just do your best each day.

The Questions:

1. Describe a time when you've had to deal with a difficult customer or co-worker, what happened?
2. Tell me how you prioritise work and tasks.
3. Describe an instance of overcoming a problem and what you learned from the experience.

4. Tell me about a time you had to work as part of a team to achieve an important goal.
5. This role requires an IT literate individual. How comfortable are you using modern technology?
6. What was your least favourite aspect of your last position?
7. What did you enjoy the most about your last position?
8. Do you have any interests or pursuits outside of work?
9. What are your weaknesses?
10. Why did you leave your last job/organisation?
11. What are three positive things your last boss would say about you?
12. Out of all the other candidates, why should we hire you?
13. What do you consider your biggest professional achievement?
14. In what kind of environment do you work best?
15. Tell me about the most difficult decision you've made in the last year?
16. Describe a time you disagreed with a decision your boss made, what did you do?
17. Tell me about a time you had to reach a quick decision that affected someone else.

18. Describe a time you've had to present your work to others (individually or as part of a team).

19. You have a lot of work to complete and a colleague asks for your support, what do you do?

20. Describe a time when you've lead others/how would you describe your leadership style?

21. How do you handle stress and pressure?

For the reasons already discussed, it's important to complete the activity. For extra bonus points, practice saying your answers out loud. Compare your first day's answers to your last day's answer. You'll notice how much easier it was, and how much better it is. Another benefit is that by doing this, you'll identify where the answers to these questions overlap. This means you'll be able to see where the examples you're using cross over with others. You can put extra time and effort into developing these examples and answers. You'll be able to use them for multiple questions, should they come up. Never use the same example for two questions in the same interview though. You're likely to be asked 6 – 10 questions in a standard interview so a few rock-solid examples will cover you in most eventualities. Notice the themes in most interview questions: Customer service, team work, relationship with your boss/previous employer, motivation, time keeping and organisation, technical skills, and a few industry specific areas. Regardless of how the questions are worded, if you have solid answers prepared on these themes you can fit them to the questions asked. This is the "trick" to giving good interviews and not being caught off guard. Read between the lines into what the interviewer is actually asking you, it will usually fall under a theme you can develop a good answer for.

There are some other generic interview questions you should have a good answer prepared for under all circumstances, the above is by no means an exhaustive list. Some others that don't fit the past tense STAR format include:

1. Where do you see yourself 10 years from now? (You already have an answer for this one).
2. Why do you want this job?
3. Talk me through your CV. – You should know your CV very, very well. You'll definitely be asked this question if they believe you're fabricating anything. Don't be caught out.
4. Tell me a little about yourself.
5. What can we expect from you in your first 90 days?

After you've been asked these questions, you'll generally be given the opportunity to ask your own questions of the interviewer. You must do this. Strong language with "must do this", but it's a non-negotiable. If you avoid this you'll lose to the people who did. It shows that you're engaged with your interviewer. Even if you really don't have anything else you need to know at the end of the interview, ask some questions. The job spec is generally a 500-1000 word vague document that doesn't give you a great idea of the company culture or the people who work there. It certainly doesn't tell you the issues the company is having. Think of your own questions if they come to mind. To get started, there's a few below. Be interested and listen to the answers carefully, extra points for taking notes. You should ask 2 or 3 questions. Any more is overkill. Don't try to intimidate the hiring manager (who is likely your new boss) or outshine them intellectually.

1. What challenges do you see the department/company facing over the next 12 months?
2. What do you expect me to accomplish in the next 90 days? (Unless they've already asked you this question).
3. What's the company's/department's top goal this year, and how would my role contribute to that?
4. How has the company changed since you've been here?
5. What's your favourite thing about working for this company?

Notes are good for interviews. Flash cards work best. They're clear and succinct. Discreet enough to look smart. Concise enough you'll not be searching for information on a page. However, choose a style that suits you. You don't want your answers to sound canned or without life. For this reason, it's usually best to title the flash card with the category of question you might get asked (e.g.: customer service, team work, achievements, etc) and include the names of a few examples you could use to answer questions about that topic. Your customer service flash card might just say "Elderly customer in phone shop" for example. Keep them brief, something you can easily flick through and look at, but not something you would be dependent upon at all. This stops you from getting stuck on any particular question.

Telephone interviews. These are just interviews. They're often used as part of a two-step recruitment process, where you'll later be asked to attend a face to face interview. It saves the employer time and allows them to weed out some less capable candidates early in the process. You'll often find there is an "informal chat" on the telephone prior to being asked to attend a face to face interview. This is still a telephone interview and you should treat it accordingly. Prepare in the same way you would for an interview. It will often be less intense, but there's no guarantee. Most likely the interviewer will be fact checking your CV going over your cover letter to ensure you're a good fit for the role. Keep these documents in front of you and know them well. Treat the situation with the attention and seriousness it deserves. Answer the phone in a polite and formal tone. Expect the call. Have all your STAR answers prepared.

Assessment centres and group tasks. Assessment centres are common in two step recruitment (where you have an interview and other assessments to complete). They're common where more than 2 or 3 positions exist, or a large number of applicants are expected to apply for limited positions. You might find yourself in an assessment centre. This shouldn't be intimidating or too difficult. The company is just trying to use different methods to select the best candidates. You can think of these like drawn out interviews, so we'll keep this section brief. Here's 10 rules for smashing any assessment centre.

1. Get good at interviews using the techniques we've already discussed, there's likely to be an individual interview section.

2. Be a team player.

3. Don't chastise anyone for their incompetence. Even if they're really stupid and ruining it for everyone else. Be specific and target the idea you think is wrong, not the person's character. Don't highlight problems. Propose solutions.

4. Don't upset anyone. Be professional. Be agreeable.

5. Your invitation will tell you what type of tests you'll be receiving. Practise that type of test online if you can. Aptitude tests for your industry, maths and intelligence (IQ) tests are available for free online (always take free IQ test results with a grain of salt).

6. Engage as many people as possible. This impresses the people watching you. They're always watching you, even between activities.

7. Help the weaker members of the group.

8. Prepare yourself better than everybody else.

9. Remember nobody cares whether you get the task right in team working exercises, they're observing how you work together with other people.

10. Presentations. Presentations are their own book. Just remember, everyone else is just as nervous as you. If you're presenting to others who also have to present, they aren't paying attention to what you're saying because they're worried about their own presentation. Volunteer to go first if you can. If you're presenting alone to interviewers, bring visual prompts they can hold and look at. This helps take their eyes off you.

Assessment centres aren't anything to worry about, they're still just interviews. A screening process to assess the most fitting candidate for any particular position. Sometimes you need to treat yourself with the respect you deserve. If 4 employers are offering similar positions with just an interview, and 1 employer is asking you to complete a day long assessment centre, the assessment centre might not be a great use of your time. Only put yourself through one of these if you really want the position. They're more time consuming and less personal than interviews. The exception is if you know multiple positions are on offer. It's usually worth it. If they're being used to staff a new team or centre, you've got a great chance of getting the job without too much trouble. Try to suss this out ahead of time by studying the job description, asking your agency, or searching the jobs website for all vacancies available from that employer.

We'll wrap up this section with some timeless advice on interviews.

1. Get there early. Always plan to be there 30 minutes ahead of time. Train delays, traffic or personal circumstances can cost you a great job. However, don't check in too early. It's uncomfortable for the interviewer to know you're sitting waiting an hour and a half early. Its weird behaviour and constitutes kissing ass and trying too hard. You arrive 30 minutes early but only walk through the doors and check in 10 minutes prior to your scheduled appointment. Wait in your car or go away and grab a coffee if your too early. Seriously.

2. Always take 3 printed copies of your CV and cover letter. One for yourself, and one for the person interviewing you, and one for their supporting staff. Unless it's a very small company, you'll almost always be interviewed by two people. This way, if you dispute anything or try to sue, it's two people's word against one. As a secondary point, the main

interviewer can also have a more in depth discussion with you if they don't have to take their own notes. That's the other reason the second person is there, as a scribe.

3. Make an "interview toolkit". This is exactly what it sounds like, think of it like a plumbers toolkit that contains everything they need to complete their job. You need a kit with everything you need for the interview.

A good starting point is:

- CVs and cover letters.
- The job specification. Read through this in the 10 minutes prior to your interview while you're waiting.
- Your notes. Usually flash cards.
- Any evidence you need to back up your STAR examples. If you say you won an award, bring the award. It's not essential but it really helps you establish credibility.
- A notepad.
- A pen.
- A spare pen.
- Your laptop, if you're giving a presentation. Don't bring it if you're not. It's the equivalent of leaving your phone on the desk in front of the interviewer.
- A separate memory stick with your presentation on it, just in case.

- A bottle of water. This is more important than it sounds. Drinking creates natural pauses in the conversation which allows you to compose yourself and thoughts. It also clears your throat and helps you stay comfortable, composed and calm.

- Identification. Some companies require you to provide this just to get into their building, and they won't always tell you in advance. Bring a driver's licence or passport. If you don't have either of these, you need them. Seriously, you're an adult, you need adult identification. It actually influences how people see you.

- Proof of your national insurance number, qualifications, or any other documents you'll need to get on the payroll if they offer you the job. Usually these can be provided afterwards, but check it out in advance and be prepared.

4. Be true to who you are and what you're trying to achieve. Bring as much of your personality into the situation as you can. This will make you stand out in an important way. If the employer asks where you see yourself in 10 years, tell them. Nobody expects forever employees anymore. The one thing to keep in mind is that they don't want you to move on too quickly either. It's surprisingly expensive and time consuming to hire people. Make sure you give them the impression you'll be in your new position for a few years.

5. Dress for success. Sounds obvious. It is obvious. I've interviewed people for £40K jobs who've

turned up wearing a t-shirt and jeans. Instant rejection. This isn't a joke. Some people just don't get it. Even if you've been at your current company a long time and you and the hiring manager are best buddies, in a super progressive company. It doesn't matter. Put some smart clothes on and have some respect for the process. Dress your absolute best with no exceptions. You're not Steve Jobs yet pal. Dress smart. Be clean. Smell nice.

6. Use people's names. Write them down at your first opportunity. Address the interviewer(s) by name. When you leave, thank them by name.

7. Maintain eye contact. This is very challenging for a lot of people. Practise talking while looking at yourself in the mirror. Tell a friend you need to practice making eye contact while giving interview answers. Try to get naturally comfortable looking at the interviewer while you talk, and *especially* while they talk. It shows you're paying attention and giving them respect. You can try looking at the bridge of their nose if you can't manage it directly, most people can't tell unless you're at a real angle to them. You can also try looking into a different eye every 5-7 seconds, this works as long as you're around 1.5meters (5ft)+ away from the other person. Break eye contact regularly enough but make it clear you're not focused on anything else in the room. You're in the moment,

paying attention to the interviewer. Look to the side of the person or above them to insinuate that you're thinking. Look down to review notes or to drink water only if you can. Looking down too much can suggest insecurity. Usually there's two people interviewing you, so you'll naturally alternate between looking at each person. This makes things much more comfortable. Looking at one person too much? Look at the other person for a while. Repeat. Don't over think this point, the main thing is to pay proper attention to the person interviewing you. You also come across as confident and capable by giving proper eye contact, which makes you more likely to get the job.

8. Stay positive. Seriously, don't trash your old employer or complain about things, ever. Be pragmatic and serious where appropriate, but not negative. It makes you look terrible. Nobody wants to work with someone who complains all the time. It's boring and brings everyone else down. Positivity is infectious, if you're optimistic and appropriately energised, it will spread to the person you're talking to. Remember: "They may forget what you said, but they will never forget how you made them feel." - Carl W. Buehner.

9. Follow up. This will help you stand out from the crowd.

Collect business cards from the people interviewing you. Ask for an email address you can use to get in touch. Failing that, look up their names on LinkedIn and find some contact details. Contact your agency or the company reception for the interviewers contact details as another alternative. Get their details. Send them a personalised thank you message within 24 hours of the interview. Keep it brief but make it specific. No copy and paste for every job, it will only take you 10 minutes and could land you a job worth a lot of money to you. A good general format is to address them by name, compliment something specific about their interview technique, reinforce why you're the right person for the job, sincerely compliment the company in a specific way, thank them and close.

10. Surrender the outcome. This is really important. You've done your best. This wasn't an easy thing. Reward yourself for your hard work to reinforce the good behaviour and recognise yourself. Surrender the outcome. Maybe you got the job, maybe you didn't. You did you best. Accept yourself and keep moving forward and doing more interviews. You'll land the right job when the time is right. Always kindly ask for feedback if you didn't get the result you wanted. Move forward. The more interviews you do, the better you'll get.

Congratulations. You now know exactly what it takes to land your next job. If you've followed this book so far, you're in a great position to go out and start earning more money by manifesting your unique talents and interests in the world. What could be better than that? A final note on interviews. They get harder the more senior you become. If you're a smart person, you'll likely find you can land almost any lower level position you want. It's possible you've never failed an interview before. You will be rejected once you start playing at higher levels. Oftentimes this is just the way the dice fall, and there's chance associated with who applies for these positions and how well you stack up against them. Often, there really is someone already lined up for the position who is definitely just getting the job, regardless of how well everyone interviews. In what my parents would refer to as "the good old days", if your manager liked you and you worked hard, the manager could often just promote you without an interview. These days there are regulations around hiring that must be adhered to. The company can be sued if they don't follow these regulations. Most of these relate to giving people of all genders and backgrounds equal opportunities to progress. This is a great thing. However, some organisations will essentially advertise fake vacancies to get around the regulations. They'll advertise the position and interview for it to cover their own backs, but secretly know exactly who they're going to hire way before they even advertised the position. Happily wasting the time of everyone involved. Often, you'll never know if this is the case. However, we can speculate that some 20% of the jobs you interview for will be a waste of your time for this reason. Accept this, don't be discouraged. There truly are many great employers, the majority in fact, looking for real talent who will hire you. Just remember if you get rejected, it's ok. Keep practicing and getting better, but never take it too personally. Your next job is waiting for you, now you know exactly how to get it.

Chapter 7

Negotiations

Negotiations are essential to all areas of life. If you interact with someone who wants something from you, or if you want something from them, you've just entered a negotiation. This will be almost every single conversation you ever have, especially at work. The purpose of learning to negotiate is to learn to protect your own interests. You may even reach a point where you're able to benefit others maximally through your negotiation skills. Your ability to negotiate will massively influence your salary, your working hours and how much you work during those hours, your position in your company and progression potential, your ability to manage relationships with others, and much more. In short, it's going to affect nearly everything you do.

If you don't work on your negotiation skills, you're essentially purposely putting yourself at a disadvantage. That isn't wise and definitely doesn't fit the philosophy of this book. Whether you consider yourself an experienced negotiator or a novice in the field, you will be able to take something of value away from this chapter. We're going to run through all the essentials of mastering negotiations. Salary, working hours and working responsibilities should no longer be intimidating after reading this section. As a bonus, this skillset will work in all areas of your life. These skills will help you get a better deal on your next car or home, help you have difficult conversations with family members, and all the other areas negotiations dictate outcomes for you.

Firstly, an effective negotiation involves building a good relationship with your counterpart. A lot of what we're about to discuss is synonymous with building trust. This is because in order to reach the best outcome, the other person needs to know you understand them and are working with their interests in mind. This will make the person receptive to working with you. It's difficult for adversaries to negotiate effectively because so much of the interaction is based on emotion.

Note that due to the emotional nature of decision making you do not want to make an enemy of your counterpart. In opposition to the popularised "strongman" view of negotiation, this is not your most effective strategy. This is especially true in the long term. With enough power behind you, you might be able to bully and belittle your way into getting what you want. Eventually though, word will get out that you're an unfair negotiator and you're willing to step on people to get what you want. At this point, people will stop giving you opportunities and become unwilling to negotiate with you. So, dispense with the brute force "my way or the highway" approach. You can get what you want without making other people feel like they have no choice in the situation. In fact, you're more likely to get what you want. People will be more inclined to help and support your objectives if they view you as a fair and decent person. They will also be more willing to negotiate with you in the future and build a longer-term relationship. For this reason, it is more profitable to use a non-confrontational approach.

You're going to want to figure out their motivations. This will be your main objective at the start of any negotiation. In fact, you don't want to start speaking about money or position or the crux of the argument until you're sure you understand the other persons perspective. You want to understand it so well you can explain it to them. You want to understand their reasons for opening the negotiation in the first place and their concerns. If you book in an hour to negotiate something with someone, spend the first 45 minutes establishing what their motivations are and building a rapport.

That's all good in an ideal world, but what if the other person is hostile? Let's run through an example to take a closer look at what we've been talking about. A colleague of mine, John, asked me to attend his end of year performance review with him. Performance reviews dictated annual pay increases and potential bonuses at our company. You received a rating in the review meeting, the higher the rating, the better the financial reward. He asked me because he was worried about the outcome. I'd been working as a manager at the same company for a few years and was relatively well regarded. I was also outside of his line of management so potentially less biased. John complained that his work was never fairly rewarded and that he was tired of going unrecognised. He told me that his manager was less likely to "try anything funny" with me in the room. I found the whole situation interesting. He seemingly had an otherwise good relationship with his manager but was convinced they would try to give him a poor performance rating for the year.

The meeting day comes, we sit down in the room. I'm determined to learn as much as I can about the situation before I open my mouth, so I begin by sitting quietly and letting the situation unfold. Now I should say that I've sat in on and conducted hundreds of performance reviews – but what happened next truly surprised me. The manager must have assumed I was sitting in on the meeting to assess her abilities as a manager and felt like they had something to prove. In fact, I really was just there as an impartial witness for John, more as a favour than a formality. John's manager proceeds to rattle through an almost unimaginable list of faults which equated to absolute character assassination. The manager didn't stop for a moment to let him speak. At face value, this was personal grievance on another level. I couldn't quite believe what I was hearing. 10 minutes of this passed, at which point the manager puts some official paperwork on the desk telling John that he's not performing to the required standards and won't be receiving a pay increase in the next year. The manager looks at John expectantly waiting for him to sign the paperwork.

Before we discuss what happens next, let's pause here for a second and take a closer look at the situation. It probably goes without saying this is a poor position to be in as a colleague. It's being entirely dominated by the other person. Our colleague has barely said a word during this whole exchange. You're probably thinking, how on earth does anyone negotiate their way out of this situation?

When somebody is openly hostile like this, it's tempting to think all possibility for rapport building and fair negotiation is out the window. It's difficult to see a way forward. When we feel personally attacked it's also difficult to keep our own composure and think clearly. Sometimes the other person will even use calculated aggression as a tactic to throw us off our guard (but you can usually tell when someone's faking it). If someone becomes hostile towards us, we can feel slighted. When we sense threats, the fight or flight response is very practical. Our instincts tell us to respond with equal aggression or just walk out the door and never come back. The alternative to flight or fight is freeze. This is common when we really don't know what to do. We find ourselves unable to do anything. It pays to understand this and prepare for it ahead of time. The worst thing you can do if someone resorts to bullying or aggressive tactics in a negotiation is to respond in kind. Remember, never make your counterpart the enemy.

So, what exactly is the right thing to do? Fortunately, the colleague I was there to support was an expert negotiator. Foreseeing this very situation, John had read up on the art of negotiation ahead of time. He handled the situation perfectly.

Stay calm. First of all, he stayed calm. He made a conscious effort to keep in mind that the emotion being displayed towards him was unjustified and the fault of character flaws in the other person, not himself. This is essential in any negotiation, it's important to stay calm and collected. It allows the other person to begin to trust you too. Staying cool displays you're not going to be easily influenced or taken for a fool by the other person.

Don't speak unless you will be heard. He waited patiently for his chance to speak. John understood that it wouldn't be wise to speak before he was certain he would be listened to. The reason for this is because if you allow people to talk over you, you are signifying that the other person is dominant over you. If someone tries to talk over you, you should finish what you were going to say. Always. Even if the other person continues to talk over you. What you're doing here is letting them, and anybody else who is listening, know that your point is important, and they should still be listening to you. You're letting people know that you expect to be heard when you talk. You should pay other people the same courtesy when they speak. In doing this you'll establish a functional conversation with mutual respect. You're going to run into conversational bullies throughout your life who will try to dominate all conversational exchange. Some of these people will be charming in all other ways. It's important not to give people the impression that you will willingly let them talk over you. So, when someone tries to do this, calmly but assertively finish your point. Don't raise your voice or become aggressive, simply say what you were about to say, as if you had a right to say it without being interrupted.

Listen to the other person. During the initial exchange John had taken some notes and made an effort to understand the key points of the arguments being made against him. He didn't like everything that was said, but he noted it and listed carefully. An important part of building rapport and mutual respect is showing the other person that you have listened and understood what they've said. If the other person talks for a long time without letting you interject easily, make notes so you don't forget things. In more civil negotiations the conversation will be two sided, meaning your short term memory should suffice.

The more the other person speaks, the better chance you have of negotiating the outcome you want. Even if it seems like the odds would be against you here, that's not the case. People expose themselves through speech. The more someone talks the less concise and coherent their argument becomes. Their argument almost always boils down to a few key points, wants or demands. The rest is just filler. Even better if it's emotionally charged filler. In this filler they expose their true intentions. They will tell you what they want, although it might not be very directly. You can use this as leverage against them, or to work with them to achieve a mutually desirable end goal. The choice will be yours on that front. Just know, the more someone talks the better chance you have of figuring them out. Information about the person you're negotiating with is everything in negotiations.

While listening, you're going to want to ascertain a few things. Primarily, what do they really want? In the above example, John's boss doesn't necessarily want to give him a bad performance review. John's boss wants to exercise her power and feel in charge. She wants to impress the other manager in the room. She wants John to understand that there have been some problems with his performance. So, although it's framed from the perspective that the outcome of the review is the only thing that will satisfy John's manager, that's not the case. John's manager wants his real motivations and concerns addressed. You can use this knowledge to negotiate a solution that gives the other person a fair amount of what they want, while critically also giving you what you want. We'll see an example of this below.

You're also going to want to try and figure out what they don't want. Use your existing knowledge and ask probing questions to get to the bottom of it. Pay attention to the things the other person is avoiding. In the lead up to the performance review, the manager had never taken any official action against John. She hadn't addressed her concerns in any meaningful way. This manager was also short staffed, 3 of their 12 team members had left within the last 3 months. This tells us the manager doesn't actually want John to leave. The company also had very long and drawn out procedures for firing anybody. They were put in place following many successful lawsuits against the company for wrongful dismissal. Employment law in the UK is strict and offers incredible protections for those with full-time employment contracts. This information tells us that John's manager doesn't actually want to fire John. All of this information is leverage.

Look for common ground and gain agreement from your counterpart before asking for what you want. You need the other person to know you've understood their perspective, or they won't make an effort to understand yours. They'll likely just keep pushing their own agenda. By showing understanding, you let them know that they've already made their point. This reassures the other person and allows them to relax. They'll also feel more inclined to actually listen to you, since you've already established that you expect to be heard when you speak and have made an active effort to understand the other person.

With all this in mind, let's revisit the conversation. We pick up in that tense room. The performance review papers are on the desk, John's manager looking serious, with faint undertones of being pretty pleased with themselves. John chooses his next words carefully, "I want to make sure we both understand each other so that I can best learn from what you've told me today". He's deliberately chosen words that re-open the conversation without inflaming the situation. He goes on to summarise the manager's criticisms in three or four sentences and asks, "would you agree these are your main concerns?". The manager nods their head in agreement. John has succeeded in finding common ground and showing understanding of the other person's perspective. From this place, a more reasonable discussion can take place. The manager is receptive to John's speech. What's more, because John has taken on board what's been said and provided a thoughtful response without any aggression, the room is now a calmer place. If you're curious, he used a confident, smooth and calm tone for effect too. He told me he used to use it to calm his children down when they threw tantrums and later found it worked with almost everyone.

Next, John starts discussing the manager's true intentions and motivations in a positive guise. "I know you're looking for improvements from me" he says. Only once things are calm, and rapport established does he start to explain how his manager's actions might negatively affect the outcome they're looking for. "How am I meant to feel valued and motivated in the team with a performance appraisal like this" John asks, sincerely and calmly without an ounce of condescension in his voice. This open-ended question is essentially letting the other person know "If I agree to what you're asking right now, there will be negative consequences for you in the future." You can't say it like that because it will elicit a negative response in the other person. You need to ask them a question that leads them to the conclusion on their own. John's manager starts trying to think clearly for the first time during the exchange. After some consideration, they responded by saying "I need to be fair in my appraisals..." and went on to explain they couldn't be seen to give special treatment.

The word fair is going to be used a lot during negotiations. Often the phrase will be used to manipulate, with no real intentions of being fair. Under these circumstances the best thing to do is bring the conversation back to the truth by turning the phrase back towards the other person. "It's important to me that the outcome of this meeting is fair".

John responded by showing more understanding, then stating "I can see your predicament. You need me to improve and can't be seen to be giving me any special treatment in the team". "Based on the issues we've discussed, I can't be certain this appraisal would be seen as fair if judged by the standards of the company." "If we can't find a mutually agreeable solution today, I'm going to suggest we both present our evidence to the area director to settle any differences." He is undermining the validity of the managers emotional argument and questioning the non-existent evidence available for backing up the rating. This was done in the same calm and smooth tone John has used throughout the discussion. There is no condescension. John is coming across as genuine with a sincere desire to reach a mutually agreeable outcome. People don't always respond to exactly what you say, they're often responding to how you make them feel. Although John's words are challenging the manager, it's done in a respectful non-threatening way. His words are very matter of fact and said with the cool self-assurance of someone who has the authority to speak on the topic. It's the "That's just how it is" when your maths teacher explains that 5x5=25. Not the "That's just how it is" when your parent tells you that you can't do something. There's a big difference.

John's manager isn't an idiot. They don't want to lose favour with senior management, they don't want to be seen giving unfair ratings, they don't want John to leave. In their emotional attack on John, they couldn't see these things. John has calmly brought all these facts into the manager's consciousness and subtly asked her to consider all of these problems, along with all the problems she has with John, before reaching a conclusion. John's also put doubt in her head about the validity of her arguments without making her feel stupid or backing her into a corner. He has used the knowledge acquired from her during the conversation, along with all the prior knowledge he had to do this.

Critically, he hasn't said much. John has made a few key statements and let them sit in the room. He hasn't felt the need to become defensive or talk too much. This adds weight to the words that do come out because there are so few, therefore they must be important. The fact you're comfortable letting your statements sit in the room without constantly explaining yourself makes the other person think you're speaking with authority. This makes them more likely to take what you're saying seriously. It also gives them time to carefully think over what you're saying, which is a big win for you.

John's manager is looking less pleased with herself at this point, but she's calmed down and is no longer angry. John has taken her from a place of emotional turmoil and brought her back to a place of emotional stability. This emotional journey wins John favour as a good person in the manager's unconscious mind. A slight crack in her composure also shows that self-consciousness of her prior outburst is setting in. She says "I can see why you think this might be unfair, but I don't know what you want me to do about it John."

As we've discussed, the point at which your counterpart starts to genuinely agree with your input is the best place to start the real negotiation. Although it isn't obvious, the manager has made a large concession in their last statement. They've gone from an explosive outburst and demanding a signature, all the way to indirectly asking John for a solution to the problem. Casually sliding the papers in front of him back across the desk, he states "I really appreciate your understanding and I believe we can reach a mutually agreeable solution without involving anybody else". You could tell she was listening at this point. John used this line to reopen the discussion. In his usual tone, he goes on, "I'm happy to take away your points from today's meeting. I suggest we work together to make an informal plan to address the points you've made." This is addressing the managers concerns and giving them a sufficient amount of what they want, a submission from John and a commitment to improvement. In the same breath he finally shows his hand and asks for something for the first time "Would you be willing to work with me to make these improvements, and would you feel it was fair to review my performance rating in light of our newfound understanding and mutual agreement?".

John has made his point. He doesn't say anything else and waits patiently for a response. His manager takes a long look at the papers that are now in front of her. She tells John she needs some time to think things over and closes the meeting. John shakes her hand and leaves graciously.

They've parted on good terms and he's made her feel valued. With John out the room, the manager turns to me and asks what I would do in her situation. I told her I would do what I thought was best for the company and in the interests of maintaining a long-term relationship with a valued employee. We part ways. John was called into her office the following morning. After their meeting, he finds me and informs me that his manager changed his performance rating and awarded him a 5% pay increase. I shook his hand in admiration.

So, what can we learn from John? The key lessons are summarised below:

1. Never react emotionally to your counterpart during a negotiation. You gain nothing from sinking to their level, and everything from remaining calm and composed.

2. Build rapport by showing understanding. Even if you can't stand the other person. Even if they've truly offended you. You don't have to like their perspective, but without understanding it you'll stagnate the negotiation.

3. Repeat their perspective back to them. Summarise their points. Do this until the other person begins to agree you've understood them. This lets the other person know they've effectively made their point.

4. Don't be backed into a corner. Always politely reopen the conversation when someone tries to get you to agree to an outcome you're not satisfied with.

5. Everything the other person says can be used as leverage against them. The more they say, the easier it is.

6. Don't directly tell the other person the problems with their argument whenever possible. Use what the other person has said to form questions. The purpose of your questions is to help the other person see the problems with their own argument on their own.

6a. By using questions that lead the other person to a new solution that's more in your favour, you're letting them change their mind without losing face, or imposing your will. Nobody likes having another person's will imposed upon them, this just turns people against you.

7. Never make an enemy out of your counterpart.

8. Shut up. Talk less. Make concise points and let the other person fill the silence.

9. Use a calm and compassionate tone.

10. Only propose your new outcome to the negotiation once the other person is agreeing with you and has seen the faults in their side of the argument. You need to give the person a reason to give you a better deal, by showing them your new solution is better for both of you.

Use these skills to get the results you want from people. The crux of this methodology is based on getting to the best outcome for everyone involved. These skills work very effectively in one to one negotiations. Something to consider when entering into negotiations; talk to the decision maker. It's too easy to get caught up in a discussion with someone who doesn't have the power to change anything for you. You'll see this often, it's a pointless and damaging exercise for everyone involved.

I once saw a man yelling at a young shop assistant who couldn't accept the discount voucher he had printed off the internet. The shop assistant had tried everything in their power to accept the man's voucher. It was either fake or invalid, and this had been explained to him. In either case, yelling at the shop assistant was entirely pointless. On a separate occasion, a man next to me in a café was on the phone to his credit card company complaining that he couldn't use his credit card in that particular café. In case it needs to be said, the café decides which methods of payment they want to accept when they choose their payment providers. Credit card companies don't go around enforcing businesses to take their brand of credit card as payment. These examples might seem comically obvious, but the point remains, don't waste time trying to negotiate with people who can't fix your problem. If your senior manager is the only person who can approve a pay increase, don't waste too much time and energy trying to negotiate with anyone less senior than that. They can't help you even if they really want to. Unless they're just as effective at negotiating as you are, they'll likely fail in their negotiation with the real decision maker. Whenever you can, cut out the middleman in any negotiation.

We need to discuss leverage. When you're negotiating with anyone, you need to be able to walk away without giving the other person what they want. If you can't do that, you lose. The person who wins is usually the person who doesn't need to win. Here's a tangible example; imagine you're trying to negotiate a salary increase with your boss.

In the first example, you really need the extra money to feed your family. Your kids have just started school and it's expensive. Times are hard. This job is the best employment prospect you have and without it, you're going to struggle. Your boss needs you in your current position. You're a valuable employee. However, she knows how much you need this job. Your boss is 95% certain you won't leave or complain much (cause negative repercussions for her) if they don't give you what you want.

In the second example, you've got a solid job offer from another company in a similar position that pays you several thousand more than your current job. You don't really need the money and have a solid offer of more anyway. Same situation, your boss needs you in your current position and you're a valuable employee. Only this time, she's 95% certain you'll leave (cause negative repercussions for her) if she doesn't give you what you want.

In which example are you more likely to get the pay increase? Clearly, it's example 2. This is the power of leverage. You need to be able to say no to other people's expectations if you want them to change. A real "no" in a negotiation means that there will be negative repercussions for your counterpart if they don't give you what you want. In the example above, "no" means; No, I won't keep working (providing my services) for you unless you pay me what I'm worth. I know how much I'm worth because another person has offered to pay me "X" thousand more for my services.

Lining up another job at your current level is the most straightforward way to incorporate leverage into a pay rise negotiation. If you can't get the money you want, you can just leave. It's a win-win for you. Note that going to the effort of this is only generally worth doing if you love your current job and employer and plan to stay there longer term. Otherwise, it's often more productive to invest the energy in gaining a promotion that pays more in the first place, even if this takes a little longer. During the rest of the book we'll clearly lay out how to do this. However, if you really like your current job and just want more money, it's fairly simple to get an equivalent job offer from another organisation and use this for leverage. The reason being is that you've already proven you have the skillset to do the job. This only works as leverage if you're actually willing to leave.

Couple this leverage with other undesirable outcomes for your counterpart for maximum effect. Never make threats you are not willing to follow through on, this will ruin your credibility. Don't do (or threaten to do) anything illegal. In the earlier example with John's performance rating, the threat of senior management involvement and the real possibility of the manager's decision being overturned was the leverage. This worked because the manager knew they didn't have the evidence to substantiate their claims. Therefore, there was a real threat of a very undesirable outcome for John's manager. Under different circumstances, different leverage would be required. Remember though, calm and subtlety is the rule here. Don't directly make demands and threats. It's offensive, and people will start treating you like a grumpy toddler who threatens a tantrum when they don't get their own way. State your demands only after building the proper rapport and understanding; lead people to the potential negative consequences through careful questions whenever possible.

To wrap things up, it's worth noting that the art of negotiation is a deep field. There are many different schools of thought in this area. As you become more senior and deal with more professional relationships, negotiation will become more and more important. You have a firm understanding of the basics here. Of course, we can only cover so much here, so as your reading list expands it's worth spending some time on the topic of negotiation. Find a system that works for you. Use what you've learned here to get more of what you want, more of the time.

Footnote: In the years since, John has gone on to obtain a management position at a large financial firm. He no longer reports to the same manager. Although when he eventually left his original position, it was on good terms. He has excellent relationships with his team and senior colleagues, and a very promising career ahead of him.

Chapter 8

Workplace Relationships

Managing relationships in the workplace can be a tricky business. To some this comes naturally, but most of us need to put in some work to master the skills needed. Some guidelines are useful here. We generally go straight from formal education into work. School teaches us a lot but doesn't adequately prepare us for high level success. There are little or no people skills taught in schools, yet alone how to act in relation to superiors or subordinates for real success. If you act like a good pupil in the workplace, you'll be overlooked and likely taken advantage of. The workplace isn't a school but employers will generally have you believe the school pupil myth. In fairness it's not a bad starting point if you have no further experience. Though it is a bad long-term model for success.

Here's something to consider; disagreeable people earn more money on average. Initially this can be difficult to believe. When we think of disagreeable people, we can think of the angry middle age man in a bar getting aggressive over the football. Also, all of the really disagreeable people are in prison. These are the extremes though, and it doesn't mean disagreeableness is all bad. Quite the opposite. The reason disagreeable people earn more money is because they're far more likely to ask for a raise, or leave a job where they're being taken advantage of. It's really just a balance between respecting yourself and respecting your employer. Disagreeable people take less shit from others. Problems often emerge here in striking the right balance. Enough to stand up for yourself and demand what you're worth, but you're agreeable enough to get on with your work and not hurt anybody. This sounds simple, but it's all too easy to go too far one way or the other.

Generally speaking, relationships are about trust. You need to be the sort of person who does what they say they're going to do. This includes the small things. If you're on a phone call and tell somebody you'll send over a quick email after a call, send the email. People notice these things. It's generally best to somewhat under promise and over deliver. Be known as the person who always comes through on their word and people will learn to trust you. Generally, that trust will be reciprocated. Notice when it isn't, and don't be scorn twice. If people repeatedly let you down, stop working with those people. Don't lie to anyone. If they ever find out, your credibility will be ruined. If you know something personal about someone, don't tell anyone else. Again, if they find out you've been talking about them behind their back, they'll stop trusting you. This is gossiping, and nobody trusts people who gossip. There's a strong ethical argument for building genuine trust with people and not deceiving them unnecessarily, but this is a book about success. The reason to keep this in mind is that nobody gives opportunities or promotions to people they don't trust. Nobody wants to work closely with people they don't trust on exciting opportunities. This is why genuine psychopaths (who are generally very intelligent and manipulative) don't last long in any particular workplace. They have to keep moving on once they've exhausted the trust of everyone around them. With the basics out of the way, we'll discuss the relationships you're likely to encounter and how to manage each for maximum success.

Your relationship with your direct manager. This is arguably the most important relationship you have at any one time in work. A fruitful and productive relationship can make your work interesting and rewarding. Equally, a bad one can make your life a misery. This person will likely be someone you'll need at some stage. It might be for a critical reference, oftentimes it's just to move a barrier out of your way to let you do your own job. People management is the territory of great leaders who can inspire others and lead them towards a common goal. It's also the territory of fragile ego driven megalomaniacs. Know this from the outset.

Your boss is the person who has the most control over the majority of your day. You spend at least 8 hours at work under normal circumstances. You'll spend 8 hours in bed or asleep. Out of the other 8 hours, some of it will be spent preparing for work or working overtime. Your boss is a massive part of your life. They're the person others are most likely to ask for a professional opinion of you. They're the person who decides how much work you're going to have to do. They have a huge influence on your level of workplace stress. They need to be respected and treated accordingly.

A bad relationship with the boss is the primary reason people leave their current job. This isn't surprising. It's incredibly easy to develop this bad relationship too. The relationship usually deteriorates in the same way any other one would. A small miscommunication that's never corrected by either party leads to gradually increasing undermining or digs and the resentment grows. Soon, after 100 tiny microaggressions, you can't stand each other. Say your boss asks you to work late one evening. You had plans, but they tell you it's very important. You reluctantly agree. Your boss never shows you a level of appreciation that matches your perceived level of sacrifice or effort. You like your boss a bit less now. You work 1% less hard the next week. You take an extra minute in the bathroom, arrive an extra minute later in the mornings (but still on time) and push yourself a little less. This happens 10 times over the next 6 months. Your boss picks up you're not doing as well in one of your performance reviews and tells you you're not living up to the company's expectations. They even tell you that you're at risk of going down the performance management route unless some improvement is seen. You like your boss a lot less now. You stop caring about impressing them. You tell yourself you'll work harder when you start getting the respect you deserve. Your manager starts to notice you acting like this and can't imagine why you're being so difficult. They start to like you a lot less. Perhaps in their concern they start micromanaging you and this adds immeasurably to your stress. They start demanding more of you. This adds to your stress. Before long, you start to hate that tyrannical manager and now think the job is awful too. It's stressful, you're unappreciated and not going anywhere. What's the point?

Unfortunately, this situation or something similar is all too common. Often it goes much further and gets much worse. Nobody said what needed to be said early enough. Don't let this happen to you. If you're already in a difficult relationship with your boss or just want to make your current one better, there are a few things you can do.

1. Find a way to make them look good. Everyone cares about their reputation. Make them look like a good boss in front of other people. Send a note to their manager praising their efforts. Thank them

publicly in a team meeting. Do what you need to do, use your imagination.

2. Don't correct them in front of other people, ever. Consider whether it's a serious point that might hurt people around you or cause damage, if so politely correct them afterwards in private. Otherwise just leave it.

3. Don't bother them too much. People who have never been people managers sometimes have the idea that their boss has the good life, not really doing anything and cashing the big cheques. The truth is far from it; managers are busy people with a lot of stress. Find out when they want to be approached with your questions (hint: it's not all the time). Try to establish the level of authority or decision making they're happy for you to make yourself and stick to it. However, do ask for their help and advice on occasion. Even if you don't really need it, it shows you value their opinion and take them seriously as a professional.

4. Ask for feedback. You should have a monthly check in with your boss. If you don't, politely arrange this with them. Even if it's just 15 minutes. Get them to tell you exactly what they think of you and your work. Listen. Don't get upset if you don't like it. You don't necessarily have to change everything you're doing; you just have to change how they're interpreting it.

5. Don't take their mood personally. Your boss is a person too. They're stressed sometimes. They're responsible for your performance, and the performance and behaviour of everyone else they manage. If you don't stick to a deadline they set you, it's their head on the chopping board. They might be going through a divorce, or undergoing tests for an illness, perhaps their grown up kids don't talk to them anymore. Have some compassion and understanding. This doesn't mean you should let anyone treat you terribly, and yes they could probably be a bit more professional, but they are your superior. Have some understanding and don't take their mood personally.

6. Respect. Respect. Respect. Have some damn respect. Whether you like them or not is irrelevant. They're in their position for a reason and they're higher up the pecking order. Deal with that fact. If you disrespect them even a little bit, expect to pay for it. Especially if you do it publicly. If you're late one morning and shout across the desks "sorry the traffic was terrible" as if you've done nothing wrong, you're being rude and disrespectful. Yes it's awkward, but walk over to them, explain yourself and why it won't happen again, and take your seat.

7. Don't talk shit behind their back. This goes along with respect. Nobody likes a gossip and somebody

will always be willing to rat on you for extra brownie points with the boss. Gossip is a sure-fire way to make people hate you.

8. Overdeliver, but don't outshine your boss in the process. It's a good idea to somewhat under promise your delivery and out-do yourself. Just don't go out of your way to prove your genius. If your boss feels you're a threat to their leadership they're likely to box you in and hold you back.

Following all the above steps should help keep things running smoothly. Note however, that if your relationship with your boss is truly past the point of repair you should recognise this and move on. Learn from the experience but retain your sanity and your desire to do difficult meaningful work. Staying in a situation with a truly terrible boss for too long is not good for your mental well-being.

Your relationship with your senior managers. In a nutshell, do everything possible to have a relationship with your senior managers. They're bigger fish than your direct line manager and have access to more of the ocean. These people generally have a real interest in helping you develop your career and will be less threatened by you than your direct line manager. They also don't need to work with you every day, so the same politics don't apply.

A great way to open this door is to be direct. Ask for a career development conversation. They'll almost always agree to this, even if they're busy for a few weeks or months. Ask them in person if possible, or if they work in a different location try sending them an email. People love telling you about themselves, senior people are still people. Ask with genuine interest about them and you'll be surprised what you can learn and how much they want to help you. Asking for a career development talk also serves the purpose of getting your name into conversations at multiple levels of management and letting them all know you're looking for a promotion. These people may well open some real doors for you. If you give the impression you want to develop internally, within your company, you'll close down suspicions that you're looking to jump ship. This should minimise the risk of your manager side-lining you as we discussed earlier. When looking for progression outside your company, the rule of silence generally applies until you have a solid offer you're willing to take.

Your relationships with peers. These relationships are the ones that will make your work more enjoyable. It goes without saying that you want to get along with people. Be good to the people around you. You shouldn't be at work to make friends, but if you do make friends, make them in your peer group. The golden rule here is to treat people as you want to be treated. Avoid office gossip at all costs. Develop your people skills. Ultimately these relationships are important but secondary to your relationship with your managers. I say this because it's tempting to join your peers in disagreements between managers and colleagues. This is generally a bad career move. Many, many workplaces have an "us and them" attitude between colleagues and managers. It's appealing to feel like you're part of the struggle or resistance, standing up against the tyranny of above… but it's misguided and not what successful people do. Successful people are aiming to become part of the elite that others are hating, and they understand that it doesn't make sense to hate something you're looking to become. If you genuinely feel oppressed in the workplace there are constructive ways to voice this that will help your career. Office gossip is never the solution, Open debate in earshot of managers or people who will rat on you in a moment isn't wise either. You can offer to create a forum for workplace improvement with the approval of your manager if you work somewhere progressive. Or you can just go and work somewhere more progressive. The easiest way to avoid gossip and negative talks about management is to remain professional at work. Make friends with people who want the best for you, and who would still like you even if you became their superior one day. Otherwise don't waste precious time, it will end up holding you back.

Your relationships with subordinates. Sooner or later you're going to be working with people who you are senior to. You may well be their direct line manager. Treat these people well, build them up. Ultimately, they are still secondary to your own manager's interests, but you need to make them feel as though their best interests are your priority. Even better if you can truly manage balancing the interests of the people above you with the interests of those below. Make things as great as you can where you are for everyone, while not jeopardising your own success. Management is a serious business and there have been endless books written on the subject. When you get there, take it seriously. You have a huge effect on the lives of everyone beneath you. Read the books and learn from the best. Take trusted council. I highly recommend having a professional coach or mentor who you regularly check in with.

The Golden rules of professional relationships.

1. Remain professional.
2. Treat people how you would like to be treated.
3. You teach people how to treat you by what you allow, what you stop and what you reinforce.
4. Keep your word. Always. Even on the little things.
5. Take a long term view of everything. Any conversation you're having with someone is a brief moment in time. If it doesn't serve your 10 year vision, it doesn't matter.

Remember the golden rules. It can be helpful to write them on a post-it note and keep them handy. Look at them each day before work and remember them when someone tries to talk you into gossiping about a co-worker, makes an off-hand comment or does anything to upset you. Keep your relationships positive where you can. Always keep your 10 year vision in mind. Everything you're doing right now serves that higher purpose. You can go forward with a better understanding of workplace politics now you know how to handle each internal company relationship you'll face. Use your knowledge, summed up in the golden rules of professional relationships, to keep things simple and bring about the success you want in your life.

Chapter 9

Health 101

In this section we're going to discuss the way your health is linked to your success. We'll discuss simple strategies to improve and maintain all aspects of your health. We'll discuss why your health is the most important asset you have. Even if you're suffering from a condition effecting your physical or mental health, there is always room to move upwards according to your abilities. Most of us will be effected by illness at some stage of our lives, we'll talk about how to minimise the risks and manage the effects of ill health when they do come up.

Physical Health. Our physical health is essential to everything we do. We must protect and maintain it above all else. We all know this. So why do we neglect this part of our lives? All too often, it takes a major health scare or crisis for us to take the matter seriously. With health, it really is a case that we don't know what we've got until we lose it. Once it's gone, it's often too late. Speak to anyone with COPD who can no longer walk up their own stairs, or diabetes patients who have lost their eyesight, or someone who has had a gastric band fitted. This is a difficult place to be. They all have something in common though, they never thought it would happen to them. We have a survivorship bias as healthy individuals, after all, we've survived so far with our current lifestyle and are doing just fine. But as you already know if you've anxiously awaited hospital test results, or been struck down by health issues, the threat is real. The human body is a remarkable, complex marvel of the universe. Despite what the doctors tell us, it still contains many mysteries.

As a younger person, I subscribed to the myth that modern medical practices could fix anything. I smoked for almost a decade. In my head I wasn't too worried. I unconsciously subscribed to the belief that I couldn't do that much damage. If anything did go wrong, the doctors could save me, right? I was young and otherwise healthy after all. That might sound incredibly naïve, because it was. The 5 year lung cancer survival rate is less than 5% in the UK. The transplant waiting list is long, and most lung transplants fail within 5 years. In short, I was carrying out my own death sentence. I did all this with the knowledge that my own Grandfather had died of lung cancer at the age of 26. It was all fun and games until I reached the age of 22 and developed breathing problems. Serious breathing problems. I underwent 11 months of tests, scans and investigations. Every time further investigation was required. A calm faced doctor would tell me that the results were unusual, but that that test was not conclusive proof of any particular condition. On one occasion my results were sent to the wrong place causing months of delay. On another occasion I received a critical appointment letter with less than a week's notice. On another occasion a test I'd waited weeks for was cancelled without explanation, only to eventually find out the test shouldn't have been cancelled and be rushed in at a later date. The UK's NHS is a miracle, and I'm grateful for it. But that year of my life was filled with health related stress and anxiety. If it was cancer, I'd have died before it was diagnosed. In fact the only reassuring factor was that while my symptoms intensified and got progressively worse, the fact I hadn't been hospitalised meant the disease was a slow moving one. Eventually the doctors revealed it was severe Asthma causing intense inflammation of the lungs.

The diagnosis was one of the happiest days of my life and one I will always remember. The doctors couldn't say that it was my own fault for smoking, but we both knew what was happening. All the stress and anxiety, all the wasted time in the hospitals, the costs involved for everyone. My. Own. Fault. The whole process taught me some valuable lessons. It made me start looking after myself properly, that's for sure. I never thought it would be me in the hospital, not at my age, not in my state of overall good health. It was an overdue wake up call, and a lucky escape on my behalf.

The trick we play on ourselves is that in the immediate moment, it's far more pleasurable to have another drink, or puff, or slice of cake. The damage we're doing isn't obvious. It certainly doesn't feel like we're making our lives worse when we're enjoying another take away meal. But that's just the trick. It doesn't feel worse until our partner stops sleeping with us because we're overweight and they don't find us attractive anymore, or we can't play with our children for very long without getting out of breath, or while we anxiously wait for the hospital test results. There should be a label on everything we enjoy that clearly states: Indulging in too much impulsive short term pleasure from this thing will cause you pain in the long term (the irony being that cigarette packets basically say exactly that). Nonetheless, the concept is so simple and everyone intuitively understands it. You can have too much of a good thing.

The office of national statistics states that in England and Wales there were 506,790 deaths in 2013, of which 114,740 were considered "avoidable". Neoplasms, Cardiovascular and Respiratory illness making up the vast majority of avoidable deaths. All these people learned the hard way about health. Maybe you don't have to. Nobody is perfect. If we look at ourselves honestly, there's probably some room for improvement in all our lives. A good place to start is just to ask ourselves a simple question in relation to our own health - what stupid things are we doing that we know we should stop doing? If you ask yourself this, you'll realise you already know the answer. Are we overweight, do we smoke, do we exercise regularly enough, do we drink excessively a little too often, what about drugs? Ask yourself the question seriously. This is your starting point. Over the next few sections we'll discuss the basics of good physical health. You should pick and choose which areas you personally need to work on. Remember we're interested in success here, specifically having the longevity and energy required to achieve your ambitions. It's difficult to stay at the top of your game, provide for your family and keep up the repayments on the mortgage when you're seriously ill. You can't avoid all health conditions. You can give yourself the best possible chance of avoiding serious health conditions, or successfully fighting them when they do come along if you look after your physical health.

We'll start with diet. A good diet is a healthy diet. A healthy diet is a controversial subject. You'll find a lot of diet fads out there, each claiming to be the best. There are also ethical and religious reasons to adopt all kinds of diets. Those are all well and good, and you can look into those at your leisure. We're purely focusing on health for success here.

Firstly, we need to keep our strategy simple. You're a busy professional with a life to live. One day you can hire a cook to make all your meals fresh if that's what you want. For now, focus on getting the healthiest diet possible for the minimum amount of time, money and effort. Try not to spend more than an hour preparing your food each day. 20 minutes per meal is plenty. That said, you do want to dedicate 20 minutes to actually preparing each meal. Don't try living off instant meals or take away food for too long unless you're damn sure those meals are fresh and healthy.

To understand what "healthy" means for us, we need to understand a bit about how the human body evolved. Homosapien-sapiens (us) have been around for approximately 150,000 years. We developed agriculture around 10,000 years ago. Before this, we didn't farm food. We were hunters and gatherers for the vast majority of our time here on earth, and mostly gatherers at that. This means our bodies evolved to take in a wide variety of foods, mostly plant based in origin.

Essential knowledge for a healthy diet:

As a general rule, you want to try and increase your consumption of whole foods and reduce your consumption of processed ones. This basically means grouping foods into ones that occur naturally, and those that don't. Wholegrain rice, beans or fresh fish are some examples of whole foods you find in nature. Sugary breakfast cereals, chocolate bars and salami are examples of foods that are processed. This doesn't mean you can never eat processed foods, just know the difference and aim to consume more of the natural stuff. Your body responds to it better.

Aim to get as many different coloured foods on your plate as possible. Experts believe this is the main reason we evolved to see in colour. Ripe fruits, vegetables, nuts and so forth display a myriad of colours when ripe. We can detect all of these colours because for eons it was critical to our survival to detect ripe vegetation for us to survive as gatherers. We used this ability to get the nutrients we needed. Dogs don't need to see in colour because they evolved to eat primarily other animals, which are best identified by smell and movement. Dogs are very good at sensing smells and hearing movements as this was critical to their survival. You can see the colours you see for a reason. Try to get as many different colours on your plate as you can.

Multivitamins and micronutrients. A high quality multivitamin is an essential for anyone taking their health seriously. It's worth spending some money here. You want one with a high vitamin availability. Some of the cheaper ones contain versions of the vitamins and minerals that your body can't absorb. The reason this is important is because you don't have the time to design a diet that naturally contains everything you need in the right amounts. For instance, you need to average a consumption of around 0.002 grams of Selenium each month. If you don't get it, it can lead to weakening in your heart, along with deterioration of the cartilage in your joints. Don't let this concern you too much, deficiency is rare in the developed world and completely preventable. Also, a deficiency in any micronutrient can have equally serious consequences. Micronutrients also have equally great benefits, B vitamins help you extract the energy from the food you eat for example, which will keep you focused and at the top of your game. Take your multivitamins. You don't have time to worry about micronutrient deficiencies. They will help keep you in prime health when coupled with a varied diet consisting of mainly whole foods.

Macronutrients. Your macro's can be thought of as the three main food groups. Carbohydrates, proteins and fats. All calories you consume form part of these three food groups. You need a balance of these three food groups to survive. Most quick diets work by depriving your body of one of these food groups. This generally isn't a good idea for long term health. You need all three. The proportions of each in the diet is still up for debate. More important than the proportions is the quality.

Fats are important for the maintenance of brain tissues and maintaining nerves. Some vitamins and minerals are fat soluble, meaning they can only be absorbed with the help of fats. There are several different kinds of fat. The most common are saturated and unsaturated. You need both. You can generally tell which is which just by looking. If it's liquid at room temperature (think olive oil) it's an unsaturated fat. If it's solid at room temperature (lard), it's a saturated fat. Saturated fat gets a bad rap in the media. This is because too much saturated fat can increase your LDL (bad cholesterol) which is linked to strokes and heart attacks. Aim to get most of the fats in your diet from unsaturated where possible. To identify this within products where you can't actually see whether the fat is liquid or solid, you can check the nutritional information in the UK. If you live outside the UK, the general rule is that animal fats are saturated, and vegetable fats are unsaturated. The main exceptions are that coconut oil and palm oil are saturated, and the omega 3's found in oily fish unsaturated. The omega chain fatty acids are required for normal function and cannot be naturally produced by the body. We therefore refer to these as *essential* fats or essential fatty acids.

Protein helps you maintain muscle mass and repair tissues, including within your vital organs. They are used to regulate immune functions and huge amounts of bodily processes. Proteins are made of amino acids. When you eat proteins, the body breaks them down into amino acids. Your DNA is essentially a code for creating amino acids, which can be thought of as the building blocks of life. In short, protein is important. Your body uses 20 different amino acids, of which, 8 are essential amino acids. Like with essential fats, "essential" means the body needs these, but cannot produce them so they must be obtained from the diet. Animal meat, fish, milk and eggs contain complete amino acid profiles, meaning all necessary amino acids needed for normal bodily function can be found in meat, fish, milk and eggs. No single plant product contains a complete amino acid profile. It is possible to get a complete amino acid profile from eating a varied plant based diet.

Carbohydrates are the primary energy source for human beings. Carbohydrates are sugars. We run our body's and brains on glucose, which is sugar. Our brain is 2 – 3 % of our body mass yet uses approximately 20% of our total calorie intake to sustain itself. Our brains crave carbohydrates. The quality of the carbohydrates we take in matters. There are two types, simple and complex carbohydrates. Simple carbs are things we traditionally think of as sugary, think sweet drinks, a box of chocolates or some white bread. Complex carbs are the ones we think of as not sugary. Think vegetables, porridge oats or other wholegrains. We want to be getting the vast majority of our energy from complex carbohydrates. They're rich in natural fibre, and as such take much longer for our body to break down and extract energy from. This is good because it stops too much sugar being released into the blood stream at once and causing an energy high, then crash. When you spike your blood sugar, your body releases insulin to help absorb that sugar into the muscles and parts of the body that need it. Repeatedly spiking blood sugars, and a corresponding spiking of insulin levels, can lead to a resistance to insulin in the body. This is known as type 2 diabetes. In untreated diabetes, the excess sugar in the blood damages the blood vessels, particularly the small ones. Fingertips, toes, in the eyeballs and more. Which is why severe diabetics often end up blind or having amputations. Obviously, it's not going to kill you to indulge in the odd sweet treat, but repeatedly spiking your blood sugar with simple carbohydrates is a bad idea. Think about this if you're the type to sit around in the evenings munching sweets or chocolate, every single day. Or if you're the type to only eat simple highly refined carbohydrates: white bread and pasta catch a lot of us out. Carbohydrates also help us retain water in our bodies. Body builders and fitness models will often completely cut out carbohydrates in the days before a show or photoshoot to achieve a more chiselled look. This is literally achieved by the body not retaining the normal amount of water. It might look good, but it can cause serious damage to our organs in the longer term.

Fibre. Fibre isn't a macronutrient. Fibre is indigestible matter that helps other food pass through our digestive system. It also slows down the digestion of foods which contain it. Our diet should always be naturally high in fibre for these reasons. It is seriously not healthy to have food fester in the intestines for too long. It will upset the microbiome and stop us going to the toilet. For obvious reasons, we want to avoid these things.

Calories. Calories are just a measurement of energy. They aren't exclusive to food. The original definition of a calories stated that it was the amount of energy required to heat 1 gram of water 1 degrees Celsius (under standard atmospheric pressure). Our body needs energy to function, not just to move around. We need energy to keep our hearts beating and digestive systems moving. As we've discussed, we need a lot of energy to keep our brains working. You should not overeat. Everyone knows the serious adverse health effects of being too overweight, so we won't waste time discussing these. A big issue you will likely face as you better your diet is not getting enough calories. This is a real issue, which anyone who has ever been on an extreme diet can relate to. We advocate a balanced healthy diet if you're looking to lose weight, without an extreme calorie restriction as this can create more problems. Extreme diets are unhealthy, and research shows people who lose weight quickly almost always put it back on, with very few exceptions. You need enough calories to function normally. I'm going to repeat that. You need enough calories to function normally.

Some things that will happen if you don't consume enough calories:

1. Your mood will be severely effected as your brain struggles to obtain the energy it requires and your hormone production becomes unbalanced.

2. Your body will hyper secrete cortisol, the stress hormone, to keep yourself alert.

3. You will be overwhelmed by an urge to stay still, as your body tries to conserve precious energy. This will make it very difficult to do any exercise,

which is essential to the healthy function of the body.

4. You will feel tired. All the time. Your quality of sleep and time spent in deep sleep will also suffer, creating a vicious cycle.

5. Hair loss. As your body is prioritising producing proteins to keep your organs healthy, you may notice more of your hair falling out in the shower.

6. Fertility problems, particularly in women. Your hormonal balance is sensitive to calorie restriction. This often leads to an inability to conceive. Fortunately, your body will generally recover quite easily once you start to sustain a healthy calorie intake for a prolonged period of time.

7. An inability to concentrate. We've discussed how much energy your brain needs, to deprive it of this will cause a drop in your ability to focus for any length of time. The hyper secretion of cortisol will put you on edge, the stress will cause you to react to all stimuli as potential threats. This is exhausting.

With this basic knowledge of food and how it effects our bodies, an effective diet can be constructed. The aim is to consume a varied and balanced diet for optimum health, energy and brain power. The facts above can be used to do this. Don't overcomplicate your diet. You don't need to eat quinoa bagels topped with avocado and a spirulina smoothie on the side for breakfast every morning. Like all things in life, we just need to give diet the attention it deserves to get the results we want. The message in this chapter is that the body needs a few things to function properly. If we don't provide these things, we shouldn't be surprised if the body doesn't function properly. If you're tired all the time, getting sick too often or just generally not feeling 100%, write down everything you eat for a week and review it. Are you giving yourself enough of everything you need?

Exercise. We need to exercise. The body is designed to move around. When we don't move enough, we start to feel lethargic and generally unwell. The irony being that this actually makes us want to move even less, making us feel even worse. When we don't feel right in ourselves, there's a good chance we're not moving around enough. Worse, there's a good reason we feel terrible when we don't move around enough. It's our body's telling us something. We're actually hurting ourselves.

The research is conclusive, inactivity is linked to an increase risk of all kinds of unwanted health conditions. The death risk from neoplasms, cardiovascular and diabetes is far higher in those who are inactive. The message here is simple: move more. Exercise is essential to ensure our metabolic rate maintains itself, with research indicating it drops 90% after just 3 hours of sitting still. When you hear overweight people complaining of a slow metabolism, they're not lying. Being overweight causes inactivity, inactivity causes the metabolism to slow down, which can lead to an increase in weight. Vicious cycle.

With exercise, the first step is always the hardest. Something to realise, a consistent message throughout this book, is that you'll probably never be truly in the mood to do the things you really need to do - but - that you can do those things and succeed regardless. We're creatures with free will. The trick here is that the first step is the hardest. Don't try to run before you can walk. A great way to fail with any exercise regime is to start from a place of zero exercise, then promise ourselves we'll go to the gym for an hour 3 days a week. Yeah, we will do that, for 2 weeks before we start finding excuses to miss the odd session here and there. Before we know it, it's 2 months later and we haven't been in the last 2 weeks at all.

Better to apply the lessons we've already learned in the book so far. Start small, break the task down into the smallest possible things you definitely will do and build upwards. "I will turn up at the gym and walk into the work out area" once a week, is a far better goal. You'll probably do some exercise once you're there, but you recognise you're laying the foundations for success by getting comfortable going to the gym first of all.

According to the UK National Health Service (NHS), regular exercise can reduce your risk of heart disease, stroke, type 2 diabetes and cancer by up to 50%. It will also reduce your risk of early death by up to 30%. Remember the avoidable death statistics we spoke about? Exercise is a great way to get the odds working more in your favour. The NHS recommends 150 minutes a week of moderate intensity activity. At this level of activity, you should be moving but still able to talk. If you're just starting out, don't measure yourself against this "catch all" target. Compare yourself to how well you did last week. If you did 0 minutes of activity last week, doing 5 minutes this week is a massive improvement. Increasing your activities by 5 minutes each week will have you hit the recommended NHS target in 7 months. This would be an incredible achievement, and it's achievable for everyone (excluding severely ill patients approaching end of life or the most physically impaired of us).

If you're looking for a place to start from zero, the NHS provides a free "Couch to 5k" programme. It's a 9 week programme designed for beginners to build up to 5km of running without stopping. It works. I've followed this in the past myself and found it to be incredibly useful. I loved sports and exercise as a boy, but after starting my office job I found myself becoming increasingly inactive and putting on weight. The sedentary lifestyle and poor diet were far worse than I wanted to realise. I would drive to my office, walk around 50 meters from my car door to my desk, sit there all day (occasional trips to meetings or the printer aside), then walk back to my car and drive home. That was the extent of my exercise. I put on around 25 kilograms (4 stone/56 pounds) in my first year at the office. The "Couch to 5k" programme helped me recapture my love of exercise. It was difficult, but not that challenging in hindsight. In the years since then I developed a passion for body building, which I used to build up some muscle mass and eventually transitioned to calisthenics. These days I also enjoy Jiu jitsu, yoga and distance running.

Energy levels. Regular workouts will make a real difference to your energy levels. People who don't exercise regularly often believe it will exhaust them and take energy away from other important areas of their life. The opposite is true. It will increase your cardiovascular health. This means more blood and oxygen can reach the parts of your body that need it. The brain in particular uses a huge amount of oxygen to function. Increasing the amount of oxygenated blood that is able to freely circular helps maintain normal function, which becomes even more important as we age. Earlier in the book we spoke about how fluid intelligence levels peak around the age of 20 then slowly start to decline. Regular exercise is the only know prevention of cognitive decline as we age. The earlier you start, the greater the benefits.

Mood. Exercise increases our mood throughout the release of endorphins, a hormone that lifts our mood and makes us feel good. Exercise has been proven to be as effective as anti-depressants in treating depression. The trouble being that when we're depressed is typically when we least want to exercise. The point is that the act itself has a huge power over our mood. The neurotransmitter serotonin is often associated with mood disorders. It is made from the essential amino acid tryptophan, and is primarily produced in the gut. Exercise boosts serotonin production. This is not a suggestion that everyone's depression is caused by a sedentary lifestyle. The point is that the scientific research strongly indicates that depriving ourselves of exercise will certainly exacerbate any existing mood problems we already suffer from.

Sleep is essential for the maintenance of our bodies and brains. Exercise contributes to a more restful sleeping pattern. It has been shown to increase the amount of time we spend in deep sleep, which is where the body repairs itself and the brain flushes out toxins that accumulate throughout the day. Deep sleep supports us in maintaining a properly functioning immune system, controlling our stress and anxiety, and supporting our cardiovascular health. Exercise outdoors if possible where there is natural light, this will further help the body establish the proper sleep/wake cycles. Studies have found that even in people with chronic insomnia, exercise significantly improves their quality of sleep. They found moderate intensity exercise helped people fall asleep faster and increased the length of time people with chronic insomnia were able to remain asleep, when compared to nights where they had not exercised during the day.

Exercise will help you feel better and live a healthy and longer life. Without it, you won't be able to sustain the health and energy required to achieve the success you want. Start where you can with what you have. Don't overcomplicate the situation or overcommit yourself. Get started as soon as you can. Develop a routine that works for you with a steadily increasing amount of time committed to the cause until you reach your goal. It's essential for your success.

Sleep. Sleep is essential to our wellbeing, overall health and brain function. We need sleep for many reasons. The subject isn't fully understood but the benefits of proper sleep, and the impacts of not getting enough of it have been established. We say not properly understood because the question of "Why did animals evolve to need sleep" is a confusing and poorly understood topic. Speaking from a pragmatic angle, you just do need sleep. If you don't get enough, you'll suffer. In the interest of keeping things simple, we're going to discuss the benefits to it, the consequences of not getting enough, and how to establish a healthy sleep pattern.

Sleep helps us recover. It's time to rest and recuperate. We use it to refresh ourselves. We all know what it feels like to be tired. Our brains slow down, we feel fatigued. We're not as patient with the people around us because we don't have the mental energy to filter our reactions in the same way. We can find ourselves getting easily irritated. Our brains fog. Decisions become more difficult and things become less clear. Forming new memories, and memory recall become difficult - when you're told to get a good night's sleep before a test, it's for this reason. You're unable to commit new memories easily and the cognitive decline you'll suffer from lack of sleep while taking the test will almost always result in a lower score. Lack of sleep can also put us on edge because it raises our levels of stress hormones (used to keep us alert) such as cortisol and adrenaline.

Something really interesting that happens without us realising it is the phenomenon of microsleep. When we're very fatigued, it's common to temporarily lose consciousness for a period of time that's unrecognisable to us. A few seconds at the most. We just don't notice it at all. You don't close your eyes or go limp; your brain just shuts down for a moment. If you've ever been driving late at night on a long road and found yourself suddenly hitting the rumble strips or swerving lanes, you've most likely experienced this. In a study, 45% of men and 22% of women admitted to having done this. If you do notice it, a sudden head jerk into awareness is the most common way of picking up on it. We need sleep to maintain brain function. We literally cannot maintain conscious brain use without rest, not even for 24 hours in most cases. If we don't sleep, our survival instincts kick in and we're made to sleep, even if it is for a few seconds at a time.

The longest time a human being has maintained visible consciousness without sleep is 264 hours (11 days). Don't try this at home. Guinness has removed the category from the record books due to the adverse health impacts associated with attempting it. The recognised record was set by a 17 year old Californian high school student in the 1960's, Randy Gardner. During the experiment he described the effects on memory recall as similar to Alzheimers. He went on to grow paranoid and started hallucinating. Fortunately, he fully recovered soon afterwards. An extreme example, but even a small amount of sleep deprivation can have adverse effects as we've already discussed. Curiously during daylight saving time, in the spring when the clocks go back 1 hour and people lose that sleep, there is a 24% increase in heart attacks. In the autumn when the clocks move forward again, there is a 21% decrease in heart attacks.

However, getting sufficient sleep has the effect of negating all the adverse impacts of deprivation. There are also some great benefits. Sleep boosts your immune system's ability to function optimally, so getting enough of it will help us fend off the common colds and bugs that are always around us. It also helps us keep off the weight. Deprivation causes weight gain as our bodies crave additional energy to stay functional and alert. Getting over 7 hours a night is linked to a lower risk of obesity. Mental wellbeing will also be improved, from lower risk of depression and anxiety with proper sleep, to the general increased mood that comes with not being tired and irritable. Getting enough sleep also increases sex drive and fertility, which makes sense when you consider the stress the body is under when sleep deprived. A proper sleep schedule also helps to regulate your circadian rhythms, which will have a hugely positive effect on your mood and general health.

That's all well and good, but what if you're someone who struggles with sleep? We all do from time to time. If you truly suffer from chronic insomnia you need to consult a qualified medical professional for guidance on how to proceed. Keeping in mind it's very common to experience insomnia from time to time, you'll know if the problem is chronic by how long you've been effected.

In the vast majority of all cases of insomnia, or general lack of sleep, the cause is poor sleep hygiene. Sleep hygiene refers to the habits around our sleeping patterns. It has nothing to do with how clean we are. There are some useful things we can do to improve our sleep hygiene and improve the quality and amount of sleep we're getting.

1. Recognise the problem. It's common for people to say "I only need a few hours of sleep a night", when what they mean is "I only get a few hours of sleep a night, and my quality of life suffers massively as a result and I'm not even fully aware of all the ways it's impacting me". Around 2% of the population have a gene that means they genuinely need less sleep than everyone else. The chances of that being us is... well, about 2%. For the other 98% of us, we need between 7 – 9 hours of sleep

every single night. Typically, more towards 9 hours if you're a younger adult.

2. Develop a proper sleeping routine. Remember when you had a bedtime? Your parents did that so that you didn't get cranky and unbearable for them. We could learn a lesson from our parents here. The more sporadic your sleeping pattern, the more difficult you will find it to sleep, and the lower the quality of sleep you'll be able to get. A good way to guarantee poor mental and physical health is to always wake up and fall asleep at different times each day. We need a time to go to bed, and a time to wake up. Be strict with yourself, like you would be strict with a child you were responsible for caring for. No, you can't stay up for 10 more minutes watching your favourite videos, it's time for bed.

3. Keep your bedroom for sleeping and sex only where possible, or at a minimum, keep your mattress reserved for these things. The point is that you need a space that is just for sleeping. We need to condition our minds to associate certain things with sleep. Your bed is for sleeping. Do not sit on your bed and work. Do not sit in your bed watching TV or streaming. Do not eat in your bed. As a side note, this made the single biggest difference to my quality of sleep as a young person. It's not easy and will require some lifestyle adjustments,

but it is surprisingly powerful. If you have the luxury of more than one room of space, use it. Remove your desk, TV, laptops, etc from your bedroom and do all your waking activities in another area of your living space.

4. If you really can't sleep, stop trying. It doesn't matter if you need to be up in a few hours and desperately need the sleep. Get up, and move to a space outside your bed, or bedroom where possible. Do something else. Use a low-ish level of light. Reading is great. Avoid technology if possible due to the blue light or install a blue light filter app on your computer or phone. Again, you need to condition yourself to associate certain things with sleep. If you're not sleeping, you shouldn't be in bed. This sounds counterintuitive at first, after all it feels like resting should be better than not resting. Maybe, but resting isn't sleep. Sleep is a physiological process with cycles, and you do not get the same restorative health benefits by resting. This one trick will have a huge longer term positive impact on your quality of sleep. Yes, it's difficult to pull yourself out of bed and go sit in a chair and read a book. However, you weren't sleeping anyway. Just go back to bed when you're ready.

5. Reduce the temperature in your sleeping area. We evolved to sleep in nature. In nature, the temperature drops at night. If temperatures don't drop at

night, your body will have a hard time recognising that it's time for sleep. Turn your heating down a few hours before bed.

6. Reduce the light in your sleeping area. Again, it gets darker at night naturally. Since we have full control over our lighting these days, we decide when it gets dark. Make your environment darker at least 30 minutes before bed, more if possible. It doesn't need to be pitch black. Consider investing in a lamp you can use in your living space that is dimmer than your main lights.

7. Develop a night time routine that you carry out before your bedtime. Use this to wind down from the day's activities. Washing, cleaning your teeth, reading a magazine you like are all good things you can build into an evening routine. You'll condition your body to recognise this routine as what you do before sleeping.

8. Keep a small journal near your sleeping area. Write down the things you're worried about before you get into bed. Promise yourself that you will give these things the attention they deserve once you wake up tomorrow. Look through the list and ask yourself if any item is an emergency that absolutely must be attended to before you wake up in the morning. If you have these emergencies, deal with them before you get into bed. Chances

are, everything on your list can (or must for practical reasons) wait 8 hours until you wake up. When tomorrow does come, make sure you actually attend in some way (even if it's a small way) to the issues you wrote down. Otherwise, you'll learn not to trust yourself and this exercise will lose its effectiveness. This exercise works because we're essentially giving ourselves permission to rest without worrying about all the things we have going on in our heads. A large percentage of us are so busy all day, we don't really have time to think about things until we're alone with our own thoughts in bed at night. This is a quiet time without distractions, so all the things we're worried about surface because they haven't had enough attention until now. Our brain see's these things as threats, and the evolutionary wiring of your brain won't allow you to avoid threats forever. If you don't make time for them during the day, they'll get to you at night. Remember though, you're a serious person who can be trusted. You don't lie to people, including and especially yourself. So, write your worries down. Remind yourself it isn't practical or possible to deal with them right now, and that loosing tonight's sleep worrying about things you can't solve right now serves no purpose. Give yourself permission to pick them up in the morning once you're clear headed and well rested.

9. Exercise regularly. For all the reasons we've already discussed. It will help.
10. Keep stimulants to a minimum. Caffeine has a half-life of around 5 hours, meaning it takes your body this long to eliminate half the drug. Here's something to consider; adenosine build up in the brain helps regulate your need for sleep. It binds to receptors in the brain and slows down the activity of neurons, which causes you to feel sleepy. The longer you stay awake, the higher the levels of adenosine build up. Therefor the sleepier you feel. Adenosine levels decrease during sleep, resetting the system. Caffeine binds to the same receptors as adenosine in the brain, which keeps you awake. Nicotine is also a stimulant that has been shown to interfere with sleep.

Mental Health. Mental health is a difficult topic to discuss because it's so personal to so many of us. As a younger generation we're more open to talking about these things. Having mentored and coached hundreds of young professionals, I can share that these issues are common to almost everyone. If we're not directly affected ourselves, someone we know and love is suffering. There was much discussion about whether or not to include this section in the book. It's been left in because unfortunately, these issues will prevent many young professionals from achieving the success they deserve.

Let's start with the scale of the problem. In 2020, a quarter of all medications prescribed in the UK are anti-depressants. This is even more alarming, because nobody takes these drugs without careful consideration and often a lot of persuasion. The true figures for depression (the leading mental illness) and anxiety are difficult to come by, because a lot of people suffer in silence. You're not a statistic if you don't see the doctor. Mental health UK states that 1 in 4 people in the UK will be affected by mental health issues during their lifetime.

We're not interested in the societal causes here. Yes, social media puts pressure on us, life is hard, and bad things happen. We're interested in what we can do about it, if anything. The reality is that mental health issues can affect any of us, at any time. The reality is that some of the time these will be avoidable, and sometimes not. However, just like being in great shape physically gives us the best chance of fighting off bodily illness when it strikes; being in great shape mentally helps us fight off mental illnesses when they strike. We've just discussed all the things you need to do to give yourself a fighting chance physically, including eating well, exercising and resting. These areas are also critical to our mental wellbeing so we can start here, but the mind needs more than just the fundamentals.

These are a few areas of our lives that need to be in order for our mental functions to be strong and balanced. If we don't have these things, the parts of our brains that evolved to keep us alive will tell us something is wrong. This will cause us unnecessary anxiety. We're going to go through the things that need to be in check in order to give us a fighting chance.

Relationships with other people. Human beings evolved to need strong relationships with other people. In today's world we don't live, eat and sleep in massive tribes. In the past if you didn't have strong relationships with the people around you, you might die. You needed your share of food, protection and shelter. Being kicked out of the tribe was certain death. For this reason, being alone is actually painful. It's your brain telling you that you're not part of the tribe and that you're in danger. Extreme loneliness is the brain trying to make you feel like you need to form relationships with other humans, or you'll die. Although these days we can survive independently of a direct tribe, our subconscious mind will still make us feel the threat because it was true for most of the 150,000 years of human history. Our brain hardware hasn't caught up to the 21st century yet, and there's no upgrade available.

These days, society favours the nuclear family unit as the foundation for human relationships. That is (for those lucky enough) a relationship with both parents, and as a secondary, any siblings. This is the foundational place to start with relationships. If you're currently short on meaningful relationships, start here. The end point of meaningful relationships is having your own family unit, with a loving partner and children. There is no deeper satisfaction for our primal tribal brain than our own family unit. You get to decide whether you have children, but the fundamental truth is that this area of your life will bring more satisfaction and meaning than almost all other when done right. The opposite is also true. A divorce will often leave both partners emotionally burned, and at least one or both sides financially levelled. Any children involved are likely to suffer immeasurably as a consequence. I say this because having a family is not the solution to all our problems and will make things worse, not better, if it isn't done right. On balance, it is immeasurably worthwhile to work towards having a meaningful relationship with your family – but do not approach the situation with naivety.

Friends are also essential to our emotional wellbeing. They buttress us against the harsh realities of the world, they help us share the burden, they laugh with us and sometimes are even there to support us in difficult times. From an evolutionary perspective, friends also help our mental wellbeing in a fundamental way. Your mental wellbeing is strangely dependent on how you perceive your own social status. There is a part of your brain that evolved long before we became homo-sapiens, that keeps track of our position in society. If it decides we are of low social standing, it will keep us stressed, anxious and alert. It does this for the reasons already discussed, because in the past social isolation meant death. Its job is to keep us alive after all. It will also restrict the flow of feel good chemicals in the brain (serotonin, dopamine) so that we don't think we've escaped the threat of social isolation. These things coupled together are exhausting for us and can potentially lead to mental illness. Being part of a social circle is infinitely better than not being a part of one. Friends (and other relationships) help the ancient part of your brain responsible for tracking social status realise that you are in fact part of the tribe, and not at risk of death. This alone can reduce how anxious and depressed we feel.

Routines. Routines are important for all the reasons we've already discussed. They will give your life structure and make every day manageable. They stop us becoming overwhelmed and simplify our existence. You do not want to dysregulate your circadian rhythms, because this will heavily impact your mood and mental wellbeing. Read the sections on forming effective routines if you need to. It's essential to get this part of your life nailed down, and it will take time and practice. The sooner you get this mastered, the sooner everything else will start falling into place.

Diet, exercise, sleep. We've spent a lot of time discussing these, so we won't go over all the same points again. This is foundational. If you can get these three areas of your life aligned and working for you, you will see dramatic changes in your wellbeing.

Career. You actually need a career. It's incredibly beneficial to your overall wellbeing when done right. It gives you a reason to wake up in the mornings. It gives you a real chance to increase your utility to society, and therefore your social status. It is arguably the most effective way to do so, and this is especially true as a younger person. It gives you opportunities. It will challenge you in important ways and allow you to develop into the sort of person you want to become. A career is a powerful thing for your mental wellbeing and stability.

Financial health. According to the experts, money will make you happier until your household income is around £70,000 a year. A £70,000 household income is achievable in a short space of time where two people live together. It's also very achievable independently, though may take longer depending on your starting point. After the £70k mark, the increases in your wealth won't continue to correlate with increases in your happiness. This also suggests that people are less happy when they're very poor, and that their happiness stabilises once they don't need to worry about keeping the debt collectors away to pay for a half decent life. Is this much of a surprise? It pays to know the roll of money in increasing your happiness, along with areas of your physical and mental health. It buys private medical cover and pays for expensive treatments where national or private insurance won't. This could literally save your life. It pays for retreats and holidays, both of which have been found to increase your mental wellbeing. It also solves problems for you, reducing stress in your life. It gives you time back to build important areas of your life up. This isn't to say money can buy happiness, because money alone will never fill the void. It just does away with a lot of the problems created by not having any money. It's important to manage our money well through budgeting, especially at the start of our careers when we're not earning as much. Money troubles bring real stress to people every day, be in control of this area of your life. Be aspirational. Be ambitious. Don't overstate the importance of money but recognise the role healthy finances play in health and wellbeing.

Drugs and alcohol. You need to regulate your use of drugs and alcohol. Alcohol will destroy the lives of a substantial percentage of the population, not to mention the impact on their families. The following figures are from the UK and are the most up-to-date statistics available from the government at the time of writing. There were 268,390 adults in contact with alcohol dependency services from 2016 to 2017. Only 1 in 5 of those in need of treatment are currently receiving it. These alcohol dependency figures have remained relatively stable over the last 5 years. There are 141,189 people in current treatment for opiate dependencies. The number of people entering treatment who were in the non-opiate group and the non-alcohol group was 35,473. 20.3% of young adults have used an illicit drug in the past year, 11.4% in the past month. Further, 90% of the overall population drink alcohol.

Why am I telling you this? To be straight, I have no moral objection to drug and alcohol use. I believe your consciousness is your own to expand and explore as you see fit (the exception being that it doesn't make anyone else's life worse in the process). We're not exploring this to demonise drugs and alcohol. Nobody sets out to become an addict. There are reasons to become one. People deserve compassion and understanding for those reasons. This is an issue that either closely affects you now or will in the future. A very large percentage of addicts are highly successful individuals. Believe it or not, it's true. There's a stereo type in pop culture of the down-and-out looser in the gutter, and this is a million miles away from where most addicts start out. The pressure of highly paid positions and an unbalanced life can lead people down a path of dependency on substances. You need enough meaning and stability in your life to make that path unappealing to you. Mental health issues and substance addiction often go hand in hand, and it's not always clear if one causes the other. One thing we can be sure of is that issues can be made worse by unregulated addiction to mind altering chemicals. Regulate your use of drugs and alcohol. If you feel yourself becoming dependant, try to stop at the exact moment you become aware. Dependant means different things for different people. An example would be *needing* a drink, or joint, or hit in the evening to relax after work. This is the time to stop, because you have a realistic chance of cutting out the dependency before it takes over your life. If you've gone too far and can't stop, reach out for help. If you've gone too far and can't reach out for help, tell someone you can trust who isn't an addict. Based on the figures above and some estimates on the real scale of the problem, there's a good chance addiction will wipe out 5 – 10% of the population. You need all other areas of your life in order to resist the temptation of filling the void with drugs and alcohol. It's especially appealing when we've been deprived of pleasure for a long period. Don't become a statistic.

To summarise this health 101. There are some foundational areas of our lives we need to gain some control over before we can achieve peak physical and mental health. Peak physical and mental health will help us achieve our ambitions by allowing us the strength and wellbeing to keep working towards what we value. We need to be consciously in control of our routines and habits, including; diet, exercise and sleep. We need to make conscious efforts to maintain relationships with others, our careers and finances. We need to regulate our dependency on substances to avoid the temptations to get all our pleasure from these, and not from our own hard work in return for genuine value added to the world. The importance of this chapter can hardly be understated in building a successful life. Use the information here to turn yourself into a machine functioning at optimum capacity. Applied properly you give yourself the best chance of the critical longevity that is essential for success.

Chapter 10

Networking

Networking will play a pivotal role in your career success. Sometimes it really is who you know, not what you know. One thing you'll typically notice all successful, wealthy people have in common are connections. This holds true for many reasons. Primarily at this stage of your career, it will serve you by allowing you to discover opportunities for work that are only shared with a certain network. Alongside this, you'll be able to get trusted advice and council from people who want the best for you. In the future it will allow you to build great teams of people, complete your work in a more efficient manner, obtain much higher status positions and solidify any higher status position you're able to obtain, keep people around you who can be relied upon, and much, much more. The strength of a good network is endless. This is also true because you can't do everything (of course). However, chances are someone is an expert at doing the things you can't do. If you have these people in your network, you can dispense with a lot of problems further down the road.

In terms of getting promoted or finding new work; you'll find that job vacancies are known about a long time before their advertised to the general population. If you happen to know the hiring manager (or someone who knows the hiring manager) for a job you want, you have a much higher chance of getting said position. This is true because you're less of a risk for the hiring manager. Human beings crave safety and stability and we're eternally afraid of the unknown. If the hiring manager has a choice between someone they know to be good, and a stranger who sounds good on paper, human instinct dictates they choose the person they know. Oftentimes it's better if you don't know the hiring manager directly, although that certainly has equal advantages. This is true because it prevents a conflict of interest for the hiring manager in knowing you directly. If; one of their trusted colleagues, their senior manager, or a mentor of theirs highly recommends you, then your chances of getting your new job just went through the roof. You'll almost always at least be seen for an interview, where you can then use the skills acquired earlier.

It's highly beneficial to be on the hiring managers mind early in the process. People are often quick to come to decisions, and slow to change them. Imagine the following example. Your 10 year vision involves leading a large department and earning at least £75,000. You've worked your way into a lower level management position over the last 5 years. You're roughly on track to hit your 10 year goal, on the right path but your progress has slowed down recently. You're feeling a bit stuck in your current job. You've been looking for a position as a middle manager for the last year. Your applications are continually rejected due to you not having enough management experience yet. You're feeling frustrated and know if you can just get into a room with the hiring manager, they'll see your commitment and you'll have a chance to evidence your skills. You know you're capable of more but aren't getting the right opportunities now that you're more senior and the positions are getting harder to obtain. 2 years ago, you worked with a senior manager who you had a good relationship with, you kept in touch from time to time and have helped them in the past. That manager has moved to a new company now. You get in touch with them for a catch up. You discuss your career ambitions and they tell you that one of their peers at the company has recently had a middle manager leave. They happen to know that the position will be available soon. They recommend you for the position, and before you know it you have an interview for a middle management position.

This is the power of a well-connected network of senior people on your side. The above example was based on a network contact who you'd worked with in the past. We all have ex colleagues, and it also shows the importance of having good relationships with senior managers as we previously discussed. However, there are many more ways of forming network connections. You can do yourself huge favours by expanding your network beyond your current circle of colleagues. We'll go through how to do this, how to maintain connections once you have them, and how to leverage your network for career success next.

An important point to keep in mind here is the reciprocity of relationships. When using a network for career success the relationships will never be a one sided endeavour. Be prepared to offer as much value in return as you'll be receiving back. You will often have to provide some of that value upfront too, with no guaranteed return on investment. That's just the way it is. If someone helps you get a job, be sure to do that job well to return the favour. Remember that person has staked their professional integrity to recommend you for the position. If you turn out to be a terrible employee it makes the person who helped you look bad, and you can guarantee you won't be receiving their help in the future.

With all that in mind, how do we form new relationships with valuable people and build our network? First things first, your immediate working relationships in the company you're currently working are a great place to start. Relationships with senior managers in particular are useful. Approach them directly at your earliest opportunity to seek their advice and council on career development. Boom, there's at least one relationship in the bag.

Hopefully you have a few levels of management, and you should be trying to tap into more than one if you can. Your direct line manager is also a good one. However, because they're only one step ahead of you in the hierarchy, there's a good chance you'll be competing for positions at the same level very soon. They'll rightly see you as competition. They also don't have the same knowledge and experience as someone more senior, otherwise they would be more senior themselves. Keep this person on your side and in your network, but don't hold out high hopes for direct career leverage.

Next up, if you work for a large company. Volunteer on cross department/business projects. These often get the attention of senior management. Examples include charity work, the larger the project the better. Big companies often try to build their profile in the community and need volunteers to do this, see if this is something offered where you work. Always keep your ears to the ground for projects with senior management exposure and take a leading role where you can. If you can't find anything that currently exists, it's on your shoulders to create it. A great way to raise your profile in your company is through charity expeditions with public exposure. Here's a basic plan:

1. Pick a charity everyone likes, children, animals or mental health are popular. Sadly, you just won't get the same level of support for specific illnesses

or individual fundraisers unless everyone knows the person who is sick.

2. Propose a planned walk, cycle, or other activity that multiple people can get involved with. In the UK, the 3 peaks walk is popular for example. Do a google search for fundraising walks or the like and you'll get plenty of examples.

3. Plan your route. Plan your proposed transport. Plan your proposed accommodation if required. Don't book anything yet, just gather all the details. You'll also need to set up a fundraising page or similar. Plan to contact media outlets (local papers) and get their details to promote the good work you've done. We recommend you look into the topic of fundraising and charity events in more detail and don't use these basic instructions for everything, not everything can be included in this brief guide.

4. Decide how many volunteers you'll need and decide on an individual fundraising target for them all to reach.

5. Compile your plan into a basic 3 or 4 slide presentation. Keep it brief. Something you can present in 10 minutes.

6. Request a meeting with your manager and your immediate senior manager. You want both of

them in the room so that your manager doesn't steal your project and claim it as their own.

7. During the meeting. Present your plan for a charity walk/cycle/etc. You're trying to get across that you've planned everything out. The reason you've called the meeting is:

A) To ask for their support meeting transport and accommodation costs.

B) To use their networking leverage to involve other departments because you want to help bring your company together, and you feel like this would be an excellent opportunity to do so. Your other motive here is plainly to involve other senior managers and expose them to you. You want to expose them to your work, your capacity to organise and pull off large events like this, etc. You're getting your name out there and backing it up along the way.

Side note: Don't be discouraged if the senior manager isn't keen to involve other departments. This is unlikely, but you'll still gain valuable exposure in your company either way. At a minimum, your senior manager will help you share fundraising messages company wide. This will get your name out their either way.

C) Confirm all other details. Insurances that might be required, dates that are best, etc.

8. Get your volunteers together. Delegate a lot of the work, don't try raising all the money yourself or doing too much work singlehandedly. You'll also form strong networking connections with the volunteers which is valuable in itself. Make sure everyone is clear on what's expected.

9. Stay on top of everyone. Plan some training if it's an event that requires training. Make sure people are keeping on top of their fundraising and not leaving it to the last minute.

10. Actually pull off the event and raise a bunch of money for charity.

11. Publicity. Make sure you follow up with big publicity inside your company, highlighting the amount raised and thanking the volunteers. Get your name published as the event manager.

This kind of event really is a win-win for everyone involved. It's a win for you because you get to do a great thing for charity, raise your profile within your company (and possibly further afield with proper press coverage), and grow your network. It's a win for your managers because it looks good for their business area. It's a win for the directors because it makes the company look good. As mentioned, if multiple departments are involved it also helps to bring the company together. This is important to emphasise because a problem lots of big companies face is being split into department silos that don't communicate well between each other. They're also more likely to offer you financial backing (accommodation/travel expenses) because of this. Companies can also offset charitable donations against tax in some circumstances, so you may find that your company is willing to match the amount you fundraise. It's a big win for the charity you choose to raise funds for. Some might say it's unethical to raise money for charity with the sole intention of furthering your own career. To which the proper response is that you're benefiting the charity, your managers, your colleagues, you're bringing people together, you're raising money for a great cause, etc.. and if you happen to raise your own profile in the process of doing a huge amount of good, you're not ashamed and will not apologise for it.

Next on the note of internal company networking, you will find your company (especially if it is large) hosts conferences or awards ceremonies. Do everything you possibly can to attend these. Often times you'll need to ask people in positions of power to find out about these things. Other times they will be published on bulletin boards, or the more modern version would be your company's internal website. You may be asked your reasons for attending these events. If so, be straightforward and true to your intentions. You want to build your network, learn more about the company you work in and learn more about other departments and the people within them. If it's an awards ceremony, you want to learn what sort of things the company rewards so you can be a better employee. Most of the time, you will be supported for just showing an interest. Take note if you find yourself working for anyone who is trying to hold you back. If you're taking time out of your day job to attend anything, always offer to make up the hours. Never make your primary job secondary to your career development aspirations in the eyes of your manager(s).

Next up, you can directly ask to shadow other departments in your company. Be careful here or you may find yourself sat next to a lower level colleague for a whole day, with no chance to make an impression on the senior colleagues you're looking to network with. Also, there's a good chance that in the eyes of your current manager, you're going to look like you want to jump ship. We've already discussed how sensitively some managers can take this sort of thing. If you know the job position you want next, shadowing can be a great way to make connections in and around your new department. Make sure you propose an itinerary for the day yourself. You want to speak to several different managers and senior managers in the department for 20 minutes each, and spend an hour sat with someone who does the job you want to do next. You need to be clear about this in your request. You should reach out to the relevant senior person overseeing that department. Best to have your itinerary for the day dealt with by the personal assistant of that department's senior manager/director.

Networking outside your company. Firstly, we're going to talk about cold introductions, and then discuss the ways in which you can make new connections with people outside your company. Cold introductions mean that you will be introducing yourself to people where you do not know who they are, and they do not know who you are. This presents a challenge because inside your company, you'll have the advantage of a common connection and a shared purpose. With people outside your company, you're going to need to establish a connection yourself with a person you don't know. It's a valuable trait if you can master it.

Firstly, you want to nail down a brief introduction about who you are. You'll use this when you meet new people at networking events and the like. You want to get across who you are and why someone would spend time talking to you in about 10-15 seconds. You'll usually introduce yourself by name, current job title, why you are where you are, along with what you're aims and ambitions are. An example would be: "Hello I'm Moreen, I work at Luxury Motors Company as a salesperson. I'm here today to listen to the speakers talk about building good relationships. I've been with my current company for a while and I'm looking for a move into a relationship management position in financial services." That's a good start, if a little scripted. When you develop your introductory pitch, try to inject some personality in there. Throw in a passing comment about something you've noticed at the event, so it doesn't sound too scripted. You might start by remarking about how comfortable the chairs are, or how good the food is. Remember, you're trying to build rapport and connections. Practice your introduction in the mirror before attending the event. Always finish by asking the other person something about themselves. A simple "So, what do you do?" will suffice. When they answer, listen carefully maintaining proper eye contact. Try to remember their name. Continue to have a conversation about anything you like but try to establish what the other person actually does. They might have connections into an area you'd like to work in. They might offer to introduce you to someone. If they do, then they like you and are trying to help or impress you. Both are good. End the conversation with the person's name and a hand shake. Don't spend too long talking to the same person. Give the person a business card if you have one (you should have one). If your company doesn't provide you with them, consider making some up. If you're against the idea of cards, take the persons number and immediately send them a text message with your name, job title, company name, best phone number and email address.

If you're nervous and new to this social setting, it can really help to take a friend with you. This can be a colleague from the workplace if you trust them. It could be an old school or university friend. It could be anyone with a common interest in career development. This can really help take the edge off. People like being invited to things, even if they can't make it. It doesn't hurt to ask a few people to go along with you either. This will probably bring you closer to the people you attend the event with too.

Ok so you're all set to attend some events, so where should you start? A quick google search for networking events in your area will yield results. It is also effective to join organisations that share a common goal or interest with your industry or working practices in general. Speaking organisations also contain many high profile members. Due to the difficulty of providing cross culturally relevant group endorsements, I recommend searching Google, Facebook and local forums for professional organisations, young professions organisations, business groups, and so forth. They exist where you are, or in your closest town with a population of over 30,000 people.

It is recommended to keep a book full of your networking contacts, or a virtual storage method. Name, means of contact, workplace, etc. It's unusual these days to outright ask someone for a physical address, but you can usually obtain this by asking where they work. It's useful for maintaining your network, so if you can find it, record it. You should also reach out to people on professional social networking sites like linked in. People's social media profiles usually have more longevity than phone numbers or work email addresses.

Maintaining your network. Whether your network is internal or external, the key is to maintain it. It would not be a waste of time to spend a few hours each month doing this. You don't need to be in touch with everybody all the time, and it's perfectly acceptable to let time pass before making contact with people. However, the more people consider you, the more likely you are to be thought of for opportunities in their eyes. It's a fine line between hassling people and letting them know you still exist. At a minimum, you want to keep contact with everyone in your network at least once a year. A great way to do this is through Christmas cards or messages. People generally appreciate hearing good news about you, particularly if they've helped you in the past or vice versa, and most people are just receptive to a request for a catch up or the like. Though, only ask for someone's time if you need it.

While networking, not everybody is going to be able to offer you a great job on double your salary. In fact, at events specifically designed for networking, most attendees will be just like you. Meaning they'll be at roughly your level and looking for the same opportunities to progress. This is fine. You'll get to meet likeminded people. You might even meet some friends this way. Keep an open mind and add these people to your contacts. Stay in touch. You'd be surprised. If you see talent or real ambition in someone else, resist the urge to dislike them. They're likely going places and might want some company at the top one day. You're also likely to meet specialists in areas you may need advice and guidance one day. Everyone is valuable in their own way and it's important to be open minded. Does this mean everybody is worthy of the same level of attention? Absolutely not. It's important to be discerning. However, give everyone 5 minutes of your time.

Sooner or later you're going to need to ask your network for some help and support. This might be career advice, it might be putting a good word in for you when they hear about the next vacancy, it might be some specialist advice to get you out of a pinch. It helps to have built up some good rapport and a small debt of gratitude by this point. One of the best ways to do this is to add value for someone else. Here are some ways to do just that.

1. Introduce them to someone else in your network. This shows good faith in the relationship and can really help people. There's plenty of everything to go round. Don't be selfish, just start connecting people and they'll thank you for it.

2. Do them a favour. This is fairly self-explanatory, but if you can do something for them, you should.

3. Make them look good. See if you have any mutual connections and talk that person up to them. Tell them how much the person has helped you. This can go a long way.

4. Organise informal events yourself. You need a small network to do this, but it can go a long way to having people think highly of you. The informal event could be afterwork drinks, or dinner. Keep it enjoyable and light hearted. You'd be surprised how willing people are to attend, even if you don't

consider yourself an influential character in your circle yet.

5. Stay in contact. It shows you value the relationship.

Ben franklin effect. This phenomenon is named after a popular quote attributed to American founding father Benjamin Franklin, "He that has once done you a kindness will be more ready to do you another than he whom you yourself have obliged". The idea is that if someone has already done you a favour, they're more likely to do you another one than if you yourself had just done them a favour. The explanation for this is that if we've done someone a favour, we must like them or we wouldn't have done the favour. It won't always be conscious thought at the time. However if someone asks you to do something, and you do it, there must be a reason you did it. The brain will fill in the gap, obviously you did it because you like the person, why else would you have helped them?

Start small. Always start small. People won't just start bending themselves out of shape to do us favours, so it needs to be something small enough for us to be relatively sure it won't be rejected. Here's some basic examples you can use in a networking setting.

1. "Would you hold this for a second?" – hand them a notepad, or anything you're holding, while you look for something in your bag.

2. "Can I borrow your pen to write something down?".

3. Once you've already asked for their details "Can you just put your number straight into my phone?".

Get creative. You're not looking to seriously inconvenience people here. Research shows that next time you really need something, you'll be more likely to get it. On the note of asking for favours, you can also ask for advice after the initial encounter. Asking for reading recommendations or the like is a great way to ask for a favour and make someone feel like you value their opinion. It serves as a useful opener or reason for getting back in touch with someone too.

One final note on this, you should return the favour at some point. At your leisure, and certainly not there and then. Just don't let it go unnoticed. If someone lends you a pen at a conference, you might cite that kindness in an email a few weeks later. In the email you might include a link to an article you liked. You shouldn't make a big deal or even necessarily mention that you're returning a favour, just try to add a small amount of value for that person in return at some point. Remember, you're trying to build a long term network here.

Use your network to land your next position. At some point, you're going to need to call in this big favour. The objective here is to have someone directly consider you for a position, or put in a glowing recommendation to a hiring manager that you get a certain position. This isn't as daunting as it seems. People are generally willing to help, the more senior they are, the more this generally applies. Start out by shortlisting your network contacts into the ones that are connected to the areas or companies you'd like to progress within. Next, shortlist by seniority. You'll want people who will be at least one pay grade higher than the position you're looking for next. This isn't always an exact science, so make a best guess. You should now have a list of senior professionals who should be able to help you make your next career move. You'll also have a list of more junior professionals who cannot directly secure your next position with any true influence. However, the junior contacts will still be useful.

Start by contacting the senior professional list. You can position the conversation you need to have via email unless the person works in the same office as you, in which case just ask for 5 minutes of their time. In either case, you want to get across the following key message. You would like to have a career development conversation with them. You want to speak to them to obtain advice and guidance, and discuss any opportunities they might know of in their business. You'll almost always get a yes. Whatever you do, don't try to have the actual development conversation by email or on the spot in person. You want to book in a time to speak either in person, or over the phone if a F2F meet up really isn't going to be possible. If you meet them in person, suggest it's over coffee. It's less formal and sets the right platform for the discussion. You're two professionals trying to help each other out. Even if the other person is senior and seemingly doing you a favour, make the setting informal. You still want to dress smartly and come prepared. If they aren't the hiring manager/senior manager of the department where the job opportunity is, ask them to make an introduction to that person. You're going to want to follow up with them and arrange a phone call.

With your more junior list of networking contacts, reach out to them to let them know you're looking for your next career move. You can do this via email. Be direct, ask if they know of any available positions in "X" area you're interested in. If they do, see if they'd be willing to put you in touch with the hiring manager, or senior manager of that department. You should have some success here, depending on the size and strength of your network. If someone does put you in touch with a hiring/senior manager, arrange a phone call with said manager to discuss the position.

The conversation with the hiring manager. You'll want to set up that phone call to discuss the role on offer in more detail. Try to share a professional story that makes you seem competent. Find out as much as you can about the position. Be polite. Ask the manager about themselves. Make good notes. If you've already come to them recommended by a senior connection, all you need to do is not mess up the phone call and you're almost guaranteed at least an interview. If you've made contact through a junior connection who doesn't have influence over the outcome of the job prospecting, you'll need to try a bit harder. Even so, remember they wouldn't be calling you if they didn't believe you were at least worth considering based on the junior colleague's introduction.

To summarise. If you have a strong network of people who are willing to help you, you'll progress faster and more effectively. At a certain point in your career you really will struggle to move any further forward without personal recommendations, and at this point you should already have a strong network in place that you've built up reciprocal relationships with. Use the strategies and advice given above to get a handle on the basics of networking. Once you're comfortable building up your network you can make the choice of whether or not to invest in more training in this area. Networking is a skill. It can be learned. You can even buy courses on the topic. Before deciding to spend any more time working on theory, it's strongly recommended to get in the field and try to make some connections at your first opportunity. You may grow to enjoy the experience. If after doing this you need some more support, know that it is available.

Chapter 11
Mentors

Mentors are a valuable source of career guidance and support. They can be gold mines of knowledge and hard-earned wisdom. The typical mentor model sees an older employee of a company providing guidance and advice to a younger employee of the company. This is a great base model and has served many people well on their way to success. There are important variations applicable to the modern world that we need to discuss. In this chapter we'll look at mentoring relationships. We'll discuss what to look for in a good mentor, how to find one (or more), the limitations of the relationships and what we can do about that.

I want to start this chapter by saying that if it weren't for the incredible mentors I've had throughout my own career, I wouldn't be where I am today. I owe each of them a debt of gratitude. I'll share a story of working for an international financial services company a few years into my career. I'd had a conversation with a very senior manager about career development, and they'd given me the opportunity to join a committee of very senior colleagues. I suddenly found myself rubbing shoulders with almost every well paid person who worked for my company in my area of the country. I was by far the most junior person involved by age and experience. I was given the opportunity in part because I'd developed a great relationship with the aforementioned senior manager over time. It was mostly down to having the right conversation at the right time. The committee itself was something the senior manager had a vested interest in seeing succeed, despite not being directly involved. I saw it as a golden opportunity. A chance to do good and display my talent in a way my day-to-day role didn't give me the freedom to do.

The committee was tasked with bettering the lives of colleagues and customers in our region of the country in a way that could be publicised. A fairly broad goal. We had a lot of scope to do what we saw as appropriate. I joined the committee in its formation and as such had input into its initial direction and focus. I've always been passionate about career development and found myself wanting this to be an area of focus for the committee. The chairperson struck a deal with me, that we could use the resources and strength of the committee for career development for colleagues in the region, if I agreed to lead this area. Needless to say I jumped at the chance. Other areas focused on charity work, some on engagement with schools, some on the large construction projects in the region. I became my company's regional ambassador for talent and development. I intended to earn that title.

Over the next few months, I worked with the committee and recruited some additional help. We all worked this committee on a volunteer basis alongside our 9 – 5's. I worked closely with the committee and ended up forming some of the most valuable working relationships of my life. My passion and energy for what I was doing came through, and it was recognised by the senior members. Many of whom went on to become mentors of mine. I was laying the foundations of a successful mentoring relationship by providing as much value as possible upfront. I was determined to show these people why I was worth investing in.

With their guidance, help and support I went on to design and deliver my first careers event. The format was simple, the first 90 minutes was a combination of me talking on stage and interviewing senior colleagues about their career progression within the company. The rest of the event was networking. We had representatives from all areas of the large financial institution come and set up stands, where colleagues could go and discuss opportunities in all areas of the company. The company provided a wide variety of financial services and employed around 80,000 people at the time. The event was packed out and successful. It opened the door to many networking relationships for all in attendance. Many,

many colleagues secured direct promotions off the back of it. It was at that moment I realised what was possible with the right mentors and networking. Although we went on to run more successful events, the first remains one of the most memorable and rewarding experiences of my time with that company.

I was 20 years old at the time, having joined the company just after turning 18. A lot of my peers saw this as a big success in a short space of time. At this stage in my career I was already in a management position and starting to see real success there too. None of this success would have been possible without having the right mentors on board. They opened the doors to that committee for me. They helped me pull off my first event. Without them and their networks we wouldn't have got anyone through the doors! They gave me the confidence to believe in myself. They deserve a fair amount of credit for where I am today. I paid them back by increasing their profiles and supporting their ambitions. This is just one example of where mentors have helped me develop.

So what exactly should we be looking for? The key to a good mentor is having them involved in your life, but with appropriate distance from your day-to-day work. The reason for this is because they're there to support, guide and coach you. You do not want it to be someone who potentially has to reprimand you in a professional capacity. Their management of you will also interfere with the impartiality with which a mentor must act. You never want to have a conflict of interest between the advice they're giving you and their own interests. This could lead to them holding you back or stagnating your career without either party realising it. This is too much of a risk in the early stages of your career.

It actually becomes more of a problem the more talented you are. A good mentor will always be impartial. Imagine that you choose your manager as a mentor. The stated intentions of your meetings are to progress your career. However, you're a valuable asset to your current team and your manager's overall team performance will drop if you leave. This has real consequences for your manager and may result in them receiving a lower end-of-year bonus or, being reprimanded by their boss for falling performance in their team. Now suppose an opportunity you would like to pursue comes up in another department. It's more pay for you and better suited to your skills. Your manager could act as your mentor and support and coach you to get that position. However, can you rely on your manager to do the right thing 100% of the time under these circumstances? This is a basic example, but it illustrates the point well. You do not want a mentor with a conflict of interest.

Next, you want a mentor who is roughly at the level you're aspiring to be in 10 years when you manifest your vision. Their salary should be equal to or above what you're expecting at that stage of your life. The reason for this is simple, it's because they've already done what you're trying to achieve. Chances are good that the person you're speaking too is observant and intelligent and will therefore be able to articulate how they achieved some of their success. They should be in a position to advise you on promotions, interviews, networking and all the different tools they used to progress their career. They should have a unique perspective on things that they have developed over time.

On the reverse side of the coin, you have a small subset of well-paid individuals who have no real interest in helping anybody else. They are self-centred and arrogant, propped up by their inflated sense of self-worth. Avoid these people. They're likely to design a relationship with you that is contingent on your success and will make you feel like a failure for not living up to their imagined expectations. They will take every opportunity to tear you down and subtly ensure you don't get ahead. They'll be jealous of your potential and see you as a threat. These people are the antithesis of professionals. Unfortunately, they're out there. They will publicly offer to support you if it makes them look good to their peers and managers. If you ever have the misfortune to encounter a fake mentor, avoid them once you pick up on their true intentions. You'll likely feel it in your gut before you can prove it. Trust your instincts.

Finding a mentor. The best place to start is within your existing network. If you have someone who fits the bill mentioned above, you can reach out to them. It's best to be direct without springing the request on them out of the blue. If you haven't spoken to this senior person in some time, it's best to open the line of communication around the career development focus we've already discussed. You can mention that you're looking for ongoing mentoring support. These discussions are best held over coffee without other colleagues you're working with in earshot. From there you can begin to negotiate the mentor/mentee relationship, a subject we'll move onto shortly.

First though, the other way to find a mentor and establish a relationship. Notably, most larger companies have specific programmes set up to match mentors/mentees. These can be great, or they can be hit and miss. At the minimum, you know that the persons offering their services as mentors are genuinely interested in doing so. This makes the approach easier. Approach these relationships with the same discerning optimism you would approach any new contact you're meeting through a networking channel. Verify their credentials and make sure they're someone worth spending time with. Don't be afraid to cut off the relationship after a period of time.

Establishing a relationship. So, you've got the first meeting in place. As discussed, the meeting place should be informal enough to put you both at ease. Coffee shops are best for this sort of thing. You're going to be working with this new mentor on an ongoing basis for some years in most cases. You want to get comfortable around each other. Dress as you usually would for a working day, if not a little smarter. Be cordial and polite. The discussion itself should be less formal than a one to one with your manager, but more formal than just meeting a friend for coffee. You're trying to form a connection with the other person in a professional sense, and you want their help and ongoing support.

Start with small talk and finding common ground with the person. Do this for at least 5- 10 minutes before getting too serious. Once you're engaged in a discussion, you can turn the conversation to your current position and where you see yourself in 10 years. You don't need to tell this person your life story, but don't be afraid to show them your self-confidence. Explain that you admire what the person in front of you has achieved. Explain you have similar ambitions and you would value their input and support along the way. Again, don't rush the process. Try to have your counterpart relate to you and your ambitions. Chances are they'll see some of their younger self in you. Just be sure to build up some rapport before you outright ask the person to be your mentor by gauging their level of interaction in the discussion.

Position the prospect of a mentoring relationship. Your goal here is to receive ongoing support and guidance from this person. Suggest you meet every few months to discuss career progression and catch up more generally. Ask the person how you can help and support them. Stay in contact and try to build a lasting professional relationship with this person. They will be able to tell you things and give you perspectives you hadn't considered. It's worth consulting them for tips and advice on finding positions, interviews and the like. Don't assume you're owed anything. This person is helping you. They have their reasons, but the primary objective should be because they want to support you and see you do well. Their secondary reasons may be because it reflects well on them during management reviews or other personal reasons. When you reach a certain level in a large company, there is an unwritten expectation that you lend a helping hand to support the more junior colleagues. This will apply to you too, so learn from the person you're consulting how to be a good mentor.

It can be beneficial to think of a mentor like a teacher. They're showing you how to do something they've achieved some level of mastery over. You would consult a chef to learn how to cook, a yogi can teach you yoga, a martial arts grand master can teach you in the art of self-defence. In the same way, it is so that a careers mentor can show you how to master areas of your career. Careers can seem too nuanced and individual to teach, but as this book shows, there are common themes that run through all careers. There are skills to master, and support will be needed along the way. It's difficult to do everything alone, your mentors will make your path easier and more efficient.

Multiple mentors. It's wise to establish a mentoring relationship with more than one person. It's also advisable to have a variety of mentors from different backgrounds, departments, companies and industries if you can. You'll need to master the dynamics of holding down a relationship with each of them. You'll need to treat them all differently and individually. A mentor from inside your company who is relatively close to your paygrade may have time to meet you once every two months or so. A more senior colleague perhaps once every 3-6 months. Mentors from outside your company and industry may be much less frequent, unless you're paying them, once every 12 months would be a good outcome.

Some people will charge you for their time. People's time isn't free. Mentors from within your company are financially compensated by the company for their time (provided they draw a regular salary and you meet during working hours). People from outside your company do not receive the same luxury. Expect to pay reasonable money for consultations with highly qualified professionals if you intend to be consulting them on a regular basis and making demands on their time and resources. This isn't for everyone, and it definitely isn't necessary during the very early stages of your career. If you find yourself stagnating and needing extra help and support, consider it as an investment in yourself and take the plunge. People pay tens of thousands for university degrees which often do not even teach them how to make a return on their money. Money spent consulting highly qualified professionals is usually going to pay off. Spending a few thousand on a career coach to secure your next promoted position, which then pays you an additional £10,000 - £20,000 annually, is an incredible return on investment in most people's opinion. Consider this carefully if you have been in your career for a while and have stopped seeing progress despite your best efforts.

Getting the most from the relationship. To get the most from any relationship you want to set boundaries and expectations from the start. You want to be reasonable but true to your ambitions. You want to get along with the person well. They shouldn't be your best friend, but you should build an effective working relationship. It helps if you're happy to see each other when you meet. The person(s) you chose should always be encouraging and supportive of your ambitions. They should challenge you appropriately, when it is in your best interest that they do so.

To summarise, mentors are an important part of achieving higher levels of success. They're more dependable and solid connections than those we merely know through our network. They are people who support us to grow and achieve our ambitions. They are people who share their knowledge and experience with us. They guide us through challenges we struggle to face alone. They're advocates for our success and always on our side. We should learn from our mentors how to be a good mentor, so we can help others in the same way one day.

Chapter 12
Staying Motivated

In this section we're going to explore how to stay motivated. Life can be difficult and sometimes this can get the better of us. We need to find the strength within ourselves to keep moving one foot in front of the other so that we can reach our goals. This journey you're embarking upon is going to be difficult. There will be massive success, and massive setbacks. You're going to encounter people who will try to take away your faith in humanity, and you will encounter people who will help you restore it. There's a good chance you'll achieve a level of wealth and success that most people in human history and across the globe today could never even dream of. Despite the success, this great life is going to make you depressed at times.

How do we stop our own negativity from levelling us out? It's a real risk, after all. It's something we should take seriously. The death of a loved one, the loss of a job we've worked years to finally attain, a divorce or break up –

especially involving children. These things can shake the foundations of the ground we walk upon. They have the power to send us down a bad path in life, away from our visions and goals. That's not something to be taken lightly. We need our world and reality to remain relatively stable. Too much instability will make us unsure of ourselves and everything around us. It will cause the parts of our brain that keep track of our position in the world to lose track of where we are. This is depressing and anxiety provoking for us.

There's a real possibility that the negative events in our lives can lead us towards nihilism. That's the belief that everything is meaningless. We all feel like this from time to time, but it's a truly dangerous place to get stuck. If you regularly feel that everything is meaningless and there's no hope, then you would be regarded as seriously depressed. You're unlikely to have the motivation or strength to get up and work hard towards your goals every day. This happens to a significant percentage of the population. It's a real problem that deserves some consideration.

It boils down to the issue that if everything is meaningless, then what's the point of doing anything? Let's keep in mind that this belief comes from a dark place. It isn't an intellectual part of us that's in control when we feel this way, even if it seems like it. It's relatively simple to move away from the "life is meaningless" argument. Imagine you're given a choice between living the rest of your life in a squalid prison cell or living out the rest of your days with your freedom. If you see any difference between these two options, there must be some meaning associated with freedom, or the lack of it. Which takes us onto the next point ignored by the "life is meaningless" negative trap; human suffering. There is meaning in pain. That's irrefutable. Everyone agrees that it's better to be pain free most of the time. People value not being in pain. It means something to us. If life is truly meaningless, we would have no problem being in pain endlessly and having the same fate inflicted on our families, because it just doesn't matter anyway? Obviously, that's a completely absurd thing to say, but it is the reasonable extension of saying "life is meaningless". So, life has some meaning, even if it is merely to be free and prevent unnecessary pain and suffering.

Perhaps by being a force for good in the world and working to reduce the unnecessary pain and suffering around us, we find the meaning in life. At the very least we can be sure it isn't the intellectual part of us that is in control when we feel like life is meaningless, because that idea is logically inconsistent. Logic is all well and good, but it doesn't necessarily help us so much when we're really feeling low. For that, we need something we can feel.

Our best and only real weapon against the feelings of nihilism is having obvious meaning in life. Your ancestors found this in religion. We modern people have largely moved on from religions, and we have our reasons. Still, with the belief that the creator of the universe had their plans for us, we were safe from meaninglessness. Without the belief in a higher power, we're on our own. We need to figure out the point to it all ourselves. That's a big ask for anyone so we should have some sympathy for ourselves here.

We've established that it's meaningful to avoid pain and suffering. However, we can do a bit better than that. One of the reasons we went through the exercise of articulating a compelling 10 year vision for our lives was to give us something to aim towards. The vision is our own, something that is individually meaningful to us. You need something to stay away from (pain and suffering) and something to move towards (your vision).

Responsibility. You will find that most of the meaning in your life comes from taking responsibility for yourself and others. When you take responsibility for something, voluntarily, you're acknowledging that that thing is important. Imagine you take in a dog (or another pet if you prefer). You feed it, walk it, you look after it when it's sick. For some reason, that animal's wellbeing is important to you. It means something. You don't want it to suffer. All of the sudden you have a reason to get out of bed in the morning. If you don't, the dog will go hungry. Nobody needs to explain to you why you shouldn't let your dog go hungry, it just means something to you that your dog is looked after well enough.

You'll get the same sense of meaning to a much larger extent if you have children. You have something that depends on you for its very existence. You understand this and it gives you meaning. To a different degree, you can achieve a sense of meaning from your intimate relationships and friendships if you take responsibility for the effect you have on others in your relationships. You can get it from your career by understanding how the work you do affects others around you and makes their lives more difficult if you don't do it properly. The feeling of "meaning" lies in all these things. The feeling of meaning, rather than the logical knowledge of meaning, lies in responsibility.

We discussed routines at the start of this book. Develop your routines for a better life. Stick at these and keep going until they're automatic and have simplified the things you do every day into manageable tasks that you complete on auto pilot. You need the essential parts of your life to run without draining you of thought power and energy. You'll need that energy when things become difficult. If you fail to maintain the essentials such as hygiene and laundry, your life will begin to fall apart in far reaching and serious ways. Your problems will compound and become that much worse.

It's useful to write your vision and goals down and have this in a visible space where you'll look at it every single day. This serves to keep your purpose front and centre in mind. The more time and effort you put into doing this, the more effective it will be. Combine the written goals with visual reminders for maximum effect. A practical way to do this is to write your goals and vision in the centre of a large piece of card and surround the statements with pictures that represent what you're working towards. Your board might include pictures of your dream home, cars you want, your family, people who inspire you to be a better person, so on and so forth. Hang this in your living space or bedroom. Don't allow yourself to lose track of what you're working for.

Consult a professional for support when you need it. Ideally before you need it. We think things through by talking to other people. Explaining our ideas helps us understand them. Have you ever had a great idea, only to try explaining the idea in a meeting or with a friend, and realising while you're trying your best to explain it that it wasn't a very good idea after all? Working through our thoughts and emotions in an honest way with another human being is incredibly valuable. It will order your mind and help make sense of the things that cannot be understood independently.

In the same vein, if you have good friends you can trust and talk through your issues with, use the relationship you've built to do so. If you can build an intimate relationship based on trust and share your thoughts, the same applies. These relationships take time to build and for various reasons aren't available to all of us all the time. This is where counselling can be valuable. Your mental wellbeing will suffer if you don't have at least one other human being in your life who you can be completely honest with. It's important. The cost to benefit ratio is immeasurable. Don't lie to yourself, you can find the money if you need to. You can find the time if you need to. Too many commitments? You're no good to anyone depressed, unemployed and unable to look after yourself. You don't just need to "get on with it". You know if you need help. Find the help if you know you need it.

Here's something interesting, there's scientific research into the utility of nightmares. The theory goes like this; your brain is running you through various disastrous situations (real or imagined) based on instinctive fears. So, if you ever have to face them in reality you're better equipped to deal with these disasters. You're also less likely to panic and become immobilised and indecisive if you perceive you've been in this survival situation previously. Your brain is trying to prepare you for worse case situations so you're more likely to survive them in real life. The instinctive fears often create outlandish scenarios, but monstrous wild attacks, abandonment, snakes, fires, drowning and loss of people or parts of ourselves are common themes.

We can observe and learn from this. There is utility in visualising bad things. It helps our survival. It's for this reason that you should consider visualising a terrible future for yourself. It will help you foresee the problems you're likely to face and deal with them ahead of time.

Much like your vision of a positive future helps you know what you're aiming towards and will make it clear if you're moving toward the good life. Visualising a realistically negative future will make it clear when you're moving towards an undesirable life.

Ask yourself; if I were to ruin my life, how would it happen? People are different here, but you already know if you really consider it. Perhaps you would be an addict, perhaps destitute and homeless, perhaps you'd let your anger consume you or another instinctive urge and end up imprisoned. There's real utility in knowing how you might ruin your life. It's not always going to be enjoyable; you may have to confront things about yourself you don't want to accept. It's an intelligent thing to explore and something that will have far reaching benefits.

When life gets difficult, it can help to slow down time. Under conditions of crisis, when things become truly unpredictable and unstable, our survival instincts kick in and make it difficult for us to see into the future. In other words, we may lose sight of our vision during a crisis. The reason is because our survival instincts are prioritising the crisis situation right now over the future. Imagine you're an earlier human in 25,000 BC. A flood has destroyed your once fertile lands and you have no food reserves. Before the flood, you were focused on longer term plans to conquer the neighbouring tribe. Under these circumstances your longer term plans have gone out the window in favour of immediate survival. Historically, in a crisis situation your old longer term plans would have no value to your survival. Better to use the energy needed to survive right now. The place you used to live no longer exists, your world has changed. The rules you used to live by no longer apply, you're in a new and scary place. Your survival instincts kick in to keep you alive, but they focus on the here and now. Minute to minute, hour to hour. There's no point thinking 10 years ahead when you might not survive the next 10 days. We faced these survival challenges for millennia.

The same neurological circuits that kept your ancestors alive in times of crisis keep you alive today. When your job is placed at immediate risk due to redundancies at your company, when your loved one passes away, when your bills are stacking up and debt collectors threaten to take away your home and possession, or any other tragedy strikes. Under these circumstances we perceive a real and immediate threat to our way of life, to our stability, to our survival.

We must slow down time. We must deal with the tragedy that befalls us in the moment. Break down your goals and units of time into manageable chunks, and measure success in micro-achievements. This is no joke. Some days, it should be seen as an achievement to maintain the most basic of our hardwired routines. In a real tragedy, it is a commendable and noteworthy achievement to stay still and not begin to spiral downwards. Get out of bed, shower, brush teeth, get dressed, do one thing to make your current set of circumstances better. Some days, that will be all that is possible. When it happens, we should have the patience and sympathy for ourselves that we would have for a loved one in the same situation. Break your goals down to this level when circumstances call for it, and reward yourself appropriately for each step you take to stay away from the negative vision of your life you're trying to avoid. Keep your vision board in clear sight to remember what you're working towards, because your brain will block this vision from your view under the circumstances. Keep your negative life vision in focus too. Think of the smallest possible set of actions you must take to stay on the right path that day. Look 1 hour ahead and define success. Achieve it. Do it again. Keep going until the weeks pass and you can begin to navigate the new landscape left behind by the tragedy. Stay on the right path at all costs and slow down time when you need to.

When times are "normal", it can be difficult to see the changes in our day to day circumstances. We must recognise our progress. Every now and again, we should carefully review our current set of circumstances. Compare these against our circumstances 1, 5 and 10 years ago. Recognise the progress we have made. Take a moment to remember the challenges and obstacles we overcame in the past. We should take an evening to sit quietly and reflect on life in a positive way. Giving ourselves the credit we deserve for our strength of character. We should recognise the mistakes we've made with a view to learning from them.

Overall, you're probably a different person with a different perspective to who you were 5 years ago. This will be especially true the younger you are. If you're reading this book as a 21 year old in university, you're probably a different person to the 16 year old you once were. Equally, if you're reading this as a 26 year old in a career, you're probably a quite different person to the 21 year old you once were. It's worth taking a minute to recognise this and give yourself credit where it's due. It can always help to think back to a time when life was tough, and things were hard. Perhaps after a breakup or bereavement. This pays because it reminds us that we can move forward and rebuild our lives. Despite the challenges and difficulties we may face, we are strong enough to get through.

Another way to stay on the right path is to give ourselves something to look forward to each day, each week, each month and each year. Try to do something for yourself, or something for the people around you, that makes you feel good. Too much work and insufficient immediate reward will lead to burn out and self-resentment. Do something small each day, perhaps you buy a coffee one day, give some change to someone in need, or talk to a friend. These small things make us feel good, and it's important to make time for that. Every week you might do something more significant. You and your partner might go for a long walk, you might make time for a lunch with a friend, you might see a counsellor. Something a bit more significant and scheduled than the daily act. Each month you might plan a dinner, or a day out, you might visit family. This should be something you really look forward to. Every year you might take a holiday, design a charity fundraiser, rent a motorbike for a weekend and take it up to the mountains. Do something significant and special that you'll appreciate and value for time to come. Of course, you should be working towards your 10 year vision, but there's more to life than just delayed gratification. History teaches us that those of us who achieve success do delay gratification, but there is a time and place for moderated rewards for our efforts. All the ideas in here are just suggestions, you'll need to figure out how to moderate your own shorter-term rewards so that they're satisfying enough to keep you on the path towards your ambitions.

Attend conferences and join organisations related to your ambitions. The comradery of meeting likeminded people who want the best for each other is a powerful thing. You don't need to meet high flyers at these things to make them worthwhile. If you meet one good person who will support you in your ambitions and keep you on the straight and narrow when you're in need, you've made the whole thing worthwhile. The main focus of this book has been raw success, this section is about staying on the path towards it. It helps to have some people you can trust around you, people you're not always directly competing with who share similar interests. You can find these people at events, conferences and in organisations. If your vision allows for it, try to spend some of your time building a network of support, not just a network of people to leverage for career success. As an added bonus, most of these events feature motivational speakers. These speakers provide temporary motivation and enthusiasm, but sometimes that's exactly what you need to re-ignite the passion for what you're doing. Make some time for this in your busy life and it will pay off.

To summarise this section on motivation, it isn't all about grinding away and hustling for hours on end. You need time and space to deal with real life too. Things will come along that you'll need to deal with, things that have the potential to derail all your positive efforts. You can succeed and prosper regardless. Keep the things we've discussed in mind when you need them, and keep moving forward.

Chapter 13
Conclusion

It's time to take the lessons we've learned forward into the world. Throughout this book we've discussed everything you need to know to start building the life and career you want. Use this knowledge. Remember to start small. It's better to start gradually than not to start. Make a commitment right now to start applying something you've learned here in your daily life. You'll start seeing improvements as soon as you start making improvements.

Lay the foundations for the life you want by building effective routines. Turn yourself into someone capable of tackling the difficulties of the world by simplifying your daily life into manageable routines. Remove excessive and unnecessary decision making in the same process. Once the day-to-day is under control, start to look forward. Cast your mind into the future, who do you want to be 10 years from now? Develop a compelling vision for your life. Develop a plan to get there, and some measures

CONCLUSION

of success to keep you on the right path. Choose your path. Hone your interview and interpersonal skills. Learn to negotiate properly on your own behalf. Manage your professional relationships with professionalism. Look after your body and mind, like they're the most valuable assets you'll ever have. Build a network of people around you to help you achieve your ambitions. Find people who have done what you want to do and make them your mentors. Pay for the privilege and the money will come back to you. Keep yourself on the right path at all costs, maintain your motivation to succeed.

Do these things to the best of your ability and watch your life transform. Your visions will come to life. You'll enlighten yourself to new, grander visions with higher goals. Keep moving forward in the world, and prosper with what you now know.

A note from the Author

I want to express my deepest thanks to you, the reader, for following this book through to completion. I hope you've enjoyed reading it as much as I've enjoyed writing it. I want to wish you all the very best on your journey towards your goals, and for you to know that I'm truly routing for you to succeed every step of the way.

If you would like to get in touch, I would love to hear from you. You can find me and my company, Occupation Navigation, on all the major social media platforms. We're always live on our website too, occupationnavigation.com.

Finally, if you have enjoyed reading this book and want to share the message and support us, you can pass on a copy of the book, write us a review on amazon, or follow us online. All of these things help to share our message far and wide.

James D. Browne

This book was proudly published by

Occupation Navigation Ltd. A company dedicated to helping young professionals develop their careers. To find out more, visit occupationnavigation.com.

OCCUPATION NAVIGATION

Printed in Poland
by Amazon Fulfillment
Poland Sp. z o.o., Wrocław